The New Perspective
on Mary and Martha

The New Perspective on Mary and Martha

Do Not Preach Mary and Martha Again
Until You Read This!

MARY STROMER HANSON

WIPF & STOCK · Eugene, Oregon

THE NEW PERSPECTIVE ON MARY AND MARTHA
Do Not Preach Mary and Martha Again Until You Read This!

Wipf & Stock
An Imprint of Wipf and Stock Publishers
199 W. 8th Ave., Suite 3
Eugene, OR 97401
www.wipfandstock.com

ISBN 13: 978-1-62032-481-3
Manufactured in the U.S.A.

Dedicated to my loving and supportive family,
Clement, Ben, and Anne

Contents

Preface

ANYONE FAMILIAR WITH THE "New Perspective on Paul" may smile at this title. How can a new perspective on Mary and Martha possibly compare with the new perspective on Paul? Granted that Mary and Martha occupy only a few verses of the Bible in comparison to Paul, their influence on women has weighed disproportionately heavy. A new look at Mary and Martha is overdue for those of us (mostly female) who live in their shadow. For those who preach Mary and Martha (mostly male over the years) the title seems rather pompous. The point—whether or not you agree with the "New Perspective on Paul"—is that as much as the theology of Paul rotated 180 degrees by the "New Perspective" that came out in 1977,[1] this new perspective on Mary and Martha is an equal shift. To women who experience the Mary and Martha tug-of-war, freedom from the pressure to choose one or the other, against one's nature and calling, is indeed a huge shift.

Can you imagine what happens when Martha is no longer in the kitchen and Mary is not even in the house? I aim to make clear that this passage is not about balancing spiritual pursuits and the practical necessities at all. That is the severe abbreviation of my findings after in-depth study that resulted in writing a thesis followed by further research that results in this book. A completely new lesson is discovered that is more accurate to the text.

I have always been interested in the female characters of the Bible, whom I found to be under-represented and misunderstood in all areas of biblical studies. Mary and Martha were the exception; they did not pique my interest. Sisters who squabbled over kitchen work and could not solve their own problems without appealing to the man in the house, sent me looking for other role models. From my earliest memory, the story did not sit well with me, except for the lesson: "Mary was the one who got it right," and my name was Mary, so I approved of that! In my adult years, I squirmed

---

1. E. P. Sanders, *Paul and Palestinian Judaism: A Comparison of Patterns of Religion.*

at being reprimanded for doing the work for home, church, and neighbor, that was so necessary and never-ending, yet that part of my life was considered to be secondary to "spiritual activities." After many "Martha" periods of my life, a good friend and pastor preached a series of sermons on Luke 10:38–42. I was fascinated by her sermons and together we started writing with the particular goal of how to vindicate Martha, who always came up short compared to Mary. When I did a mountain of research and after reading the passages in Greek and many commentaries, some unique questions took shape.

I was puzzled about why Mary seems to attract so much favorable attention, not only in recent publications, but also throughout history, and surprisingly even in the biblical text itself. Beyond two strong affirmations from Jesus, in Luke 10:42 and John 12:17, hints lie in the Greek text itself where Mary receives prominence for which there is no obvious accounting. What is this allure that clings to Mary? I looked into possible ways that a first-century Jewish woman could attain fame, a following, or any extra attention. What kind of mayor, tourist destination, miracle worker, or saint, could she have been in the first-century Jewish context? I started a thesis on a quest to discover the mystery of Mary, but I had no reason to think I would find any conclusions; I fully expected to come up empty and have to start a new thesis.

When I discovered a new perspective on Mary, then Martha came into her own light. I slowly uncovered bits and pieces from many diverse sources, which I cite in the course of this book. Most of the puzzle parts are certainly not original with me, but no one has put them together as I have. I readily acknowledge the guiding of the Holy Spirit in directing me to the right journals, conversations, and books, at what seemed at the time to be random coincidences. Perhaps I am presumptuous to think that in two thousand years of interpretation, I am the first to come up with a new look for Mary and Martha. I am looking forward to the verdict, so give this a read and you decide if the old aunts are not so crotchety after all.

Acknowledgments

I AM MUCH INDEBTED to many people for the encouragement and guidance that made this book possible. Hugs to Jean Hess, DMin. Because of her sermon series, she raised my enthusiasm for further study on the sisters of Bethany and I started to research the texts. At the time, I was a seminary student closing in on the semester I had to start a thesis. Since I already had much work done, I decided to go with a topic that had already engaged my interest with no sign of being soon exhausted. Many professors at Denver Theological Seminary guided me on the entire experience starting with Dr. Keith Wells who suggested on my proposal, "Why not consider the narrative function of Mary of Bethany?" So my thesis title became, "Mary of Bethany: Her Narrative Function." Dr. William Klein was my first reader, who spent extra time with me on the semester of his sabbatical. Dr. Judith Diehl was my second reader, who enhanced my confidence and grammar by reading the final draft of this book as well. Many thanks to additional professors who have encouraged my writing and answered various random questions including Dr. Doug Groothuis, Dr. Craig Blomberg, Dr. Richard Hess, Dr. Hélène Dallaire, and Dr. Susan Hecht.

I also thank Dr. Mimi Haddad and the staff at Christians for Biblical Equality for their huge encouragement by offering the student competition of which I was a winner and privileged to present a short version of my thesis at their conference in Seattle in July of 2011. A shortened version of one chapter of this book was published in the CBE journal, "Priscilla Papers," Spring 2012. Many dear friends have been at my side with their prayers and encouragement including Richard Craft, DMin, who read my manuscript and my fellow writers in the Denver Seminary Writers' Group.

My son, daughter, and husband, to whom this is dedicated, enthusiastically support me in numerous ways, even if their eyes glaze over at the mention of my studies. They provide me opportunity to practice much *diakonia* in home and church, as well as ministries in the great unknown after the example of Mary and Martha, who were commissioned to discipleship by Jesus.

PART I

1

Why Mary and Martha? Again?

FRANKLY, IS THERE ANYTHING new to say about the sisters? These characters have become a cliché over the centuries. The mere mention of these two names brings up visions of sisters squabbling over the kitchen work as read in Luke 10:38–42. In the Johannine passages, the sisters remain in character; Mary falls at the feet of Jesus, and Martha is not at a loss for words. Finally, in John 12, she is back in her role as hostess—this time without complaining. Martha learned her lesson well.

So I ask, "What more is there to know about Mary and Martha of Bethany?" We all have our favorite, well-worn visions of how certain biblical stories occurred. The scenario with Mary and Martha runs something like this: one day Martha opens her door to a big surprise. Jesus stands on the threshold with several disciples in tow, if not all twelve. They look hungry . . . and thirsty . . . and they need their feet washed . . . and a place to sleep . . . and what else could be necessary to provide proper hospitality for Jesus and his entourage? Martha goes into a frenzy of food preparation and sets the servants scurrying while she raids the wine cellar. Meanwhile, her irresponsible sister has slipped out of the kitchen. Gasp, of all things, she is sitting at the feet of Jesus, in the company of the men! What can she be thinking? Martha has just had enough. She pleads with Jesus to set her negligent sister straight. Jesus severely reprimands Martha for questioning Mary's place at his feet. Mary is esteemed as the sister who "got it right."

Best-selling Christian books uphold contemplative study, exemplified by Mary, and malign the practical ministry of Martha. The conclusion is familiar: passively listen more to Jesus. Do not let the mundane duties of life take over excessively to the point of infringing upon the preferred activities of study and worship. These conclusions set a dissonant tone in the minds of many women—and men as well—who have heard many variations of this same lesson.

Numerous devotions and sermons unnecessarily urge listeners into the mold of Mary of Bethany, when they may be gifted to a different mode of discipleship. These stereotypes have been so internalized that even in secular settings one can hear women exclaim that they became too busy and their "Martha-side" got the better of them. Should we all be Marys as she has been typically characterized? If Mary really exemplifies the role to be emulated, then are we teaching the lessons that are accurate to her portrait in Luke and John?

Furthermore, the traditional interpretations seem to denigrate the necessary work of women, in favor of Bible study and spiritual pursuits. Dangers lurk in the more superficial readings, which are directed primarily to women, and then boiled down—excuse the cooking terminology—to the choices women must make. Women are—yes, pressure-cooked—to prefer the "higher things" but at the same time be the "hostess with the mostest," without breaking a sweat!

When a woman fails at this super-human task, she feels "less-than." This interpretation denigrates the traditional work of women and the so-called nurturing natures in favor of more "masculine" qualities of learning and the mind. Readers may conclude that their ways of serving, and their strongest gifts are not desirable. They feel they have to give up their "lesser talents" which are essential to the ministry of the kingdom. "Consequently many women in the church, who even now tend to identify with Martha, feel that they are less valuable, even worthless, and develop inferiority complexes."[1]

The New Perspective on Mary and Martha will study the evidence and put both of the sisters into a more accurate light. A deep look at Luke 10:38–42 followed by application to John 11:1—12:11, that truly digs beyond the superficial answers is rare. Mary and Martha have been relegated to a sort of women's ghetto from which men prefer to excuse themselves. The history of scholarship on Mary and Martha narratives is disproportionately seen as applying only to women because the protagonists are women, therefore only women's applications are considered. Because only stereotypical questions are asked, then predictable conclusions are accepted. At least a generation of devotions and sermons have drawn from the same research and repeated the same scholarship.

A fresh look is overdue and a new perspective on the characters waits to be discovered. This book includes background information on many historical-cultural issues that impact the way we understand the daily

1. Moltmann-Wendel, *The Women Around Jesus*, 21.

life of Mary and Martha. A thorough exegesis of the Greek texts of Luke 10:38–43 and John 11:1—12:1–11 recovers the original story. New applications emerge creating deeper self-understanding for those who struggle with their own calling and discipleship, and in addition, the calls of those they love.

This study moves Mary and Martha far beyond the old conversations that have haunted Bible studies for centuries. The false dichotomies and forced conclusions fade in comparison to the much more important issues these women illustrate. Discover a whole new look for Mary and Martha in the narrative of Christ's journey to the cross and a more complex model for discipleship and illustration of community.

TWO THOUSAND YEARS OF MARY AND MARTHA: HISTORICAL INTERPRETATIONS THROUGHOUT THE AGES

A small excursus is necessary to set things straight at the very beginning. Martha has mostly escaped the indignity of being confused with other characters. In her favor, she is the only Martha mentioned in the Bible. It is a sad fact that Mary of Bethany has been conflated with various other Marys. Mary was a very popular name in the first century with several different individuals named Mary mentioned in the Gospels. Elizabeth Moltmann-Wendel expresses the confusion well:

"Mary of Bethany suffers the fate of many women; her voice is not loud, what she says is not original, her story is not dramatic. Her behavior is not noticeable, her conduct is modest. She seems sympathetic, but by her next entrance, people have forgotten her name and confuse her with another woman who has made more of an impression."[2]

Who's Who? A Case of Confused Identity

The best known Mary, the mother of Jesus, is usually referred to as such, or as Mary of Nazareth. Much more confusing is that in the early centuries—and yet today—Mary of Bethany is often conflated with Mary Magdalene.[3] The similarity is that both performed services of special care for the body

---

2. Moltmann-Wendell, *The Women*, 53.

3. Cohick, *Women in the World*, 318.

of Jesus. Mary Magdalene in Luke 24:10, with other unidentified women, carried spices to the grave of Jesus to preserve his body in death. Mary of Bethany (John 12:1–8) anointed his feet with perfume and wiped them with her hair six days before the Passion Week. In John 12:7, Jesus states that the ointment Mary used is "to be kept for the day of his burial." Martha and/or her sister, Mary could have been at the tomb of Jesus, but they are not explicitly named in any of the Gospels unlike Mary Magdalene.

Still more confusion between Marys occurs because Mary Magdalene is identified with the unnamed woman called "sinful" in the anointing story of Luke 7, which may or may not refer to the same event of John 12. The differences and parallels of the four "anointing pericopes" (Mark 14:3–9, Matt. 26: 6–13, John 12:1–8, and Luke 7:36–50), and the likelihood that Mary of Bethany was the original actor in one or more events retold with variations, is another key discussion which will be pursued below.

One of the earliest perpetrators of this conflation of the Marys was Hippolytus (170–235), who writes in *Canticum canticorum* 25.6 that Martha and Mary were witnesses to the resurrection.[4] There is no certain record of Mary and Martha at the crucifixion nor the resurrection, but so starts the confusion between Mary Magdalene and Mary of Bethany. Tertullian (160–225) might be the first to connect the woman called sinful of Luke 7 with Mary Magdalene.[5] He describes Mary Magdalene in John 20:17 as a sinner who had covered Jesus' feet with kisses, bathed them with her tears, wiped them with her hair, and anointed them with ointment. Now Mary Magdalene, Mary of Bethany, and the "sinful woman" of Luke 7 are all intertwined.

Pope Gregory the Great in AD 591 in *Homilae* 23, made it official that three Marys were actually one Mary.[6] He identified Mary Magdalene with the unnamed woman of Luke 7 and Mary of Bethany. "With the exegetical stroke of the pen, Pope Gregory reduced three women to one, and removed from historical record the prominent place of Mary of Magdala's benefaction of the Jesus movement."[7] This may have simplified the confusion of the Marys, but does a great injustice to each of the Marys who have an important identity in her own right. In western Christendom, Mary of

4. Cohick, *Women in the World*, 318.

5. Quote of Jane Schaberg in Cohick, *Women*, 318.

6. Cohick, *Women in the World*, 319.

7. Cohick, *Women in the World*, 319.

Bethany came to be inseparable from Mary Magdalene, although in the Eastern Church they remained separate women.[8]

The family tree was further complicated when Martha and Mary Magdalene became sisters, probably as the mistake of a copyist ca. 595.[9] By medieval times, it is difficult to determine which woman is the topic of discussion, i.e., the Magdalene or Mary of Bethany. In the twelfth century, the story is elaborated that Lazarus and Mary Magdalene—or maybe it was Mary of Bethany—had travelled to Provence after the ascension of Christ.[10] Meanwhile various legends grew around the original family members including Martha's subjugation of a dragon, a legend that spread in medieval France.[11] One sure conclusion to draw from this confusion of identification is that fascination with the siblings of Bethany has not waned throughout the centuries up to the present.

HISTORY OF INTERPRETATION

These two sisters have carried quite a burden of interpretation over two millennia. From the earliest recorded expositions, the story has been heavily allegorized. Mary and Martha are used to illustrate the active *praxis* and contemplative *theōreō* life, the present world and the world to come, Judaism and Christianity, justification by works and justification by faith, and Protestantism and Catholicism.[12]

Clement and Origen in mid-third-century Alexandria, were the first to peg the two sisters as models for action and contemplation, although they agreed that neither action nor contemplation could exist without the other.[13] Origen suggested that Martha could be seen as symbolic of the Synagogue and the Old Testament laws, while Mary represented the Christian Church and the new "spiritual law" (Rom. 7:14). Martha symbolized the Jews, who observed the precepts of the law, while Mary represented the Christians, who "set their minds on things that are above" (Col. 3:2).[14] Christ's commendation indicates the superiority of her choice, but Origen

8. Peters, *Many Faces*, 213.

9. Peters, *Many Faces*, 13.

10. Peters, *Many Faces*, 14.

11. Peters, *Many Faces*, 18.

12. Nolland, *Luke 9:21–18:34*, 602.

13. Constable, *Three Studies*, 14.

14. Peters, *Many Faces*, 13.

did not separate Mary and Martha: "Action and contemplation do not exist one without the other."[15] At the time of Origen, the Platonic influence was strong; many like him tended to see distinctions between practice and theory, and between action and contemplation.[16] These contrasts are not found in the Judaic tradition and are a contribution of Greek thought to early Christianity.[17] Origen's ideas were especially well received in monastic circles, who looked for confirmation of the spiritual against the worldly, and have set the precedent for interpretation since.

Gregory the Great (540–604) in his "Homily on Ezekiel" reinforced a monastic emphasis, which the early church saw as the superiority of the contemplative life over the active life.[18] Historically, in Catholic tradition, women had two choices that did not mix: they could practice a lifestyle of celibacy in service to God, or marry, have children and thereby serve their husbands and the world. The story of Mary and Martha reinforced Mary's choice as the preferred.[19]

In the mid-seventh century, Luke 10:38–42 became the lectionary reading for the Feast of the Assumption of Mary. Consider the countless sermons that were prepared and preached on the Latin translation of this text on August 15 of every year since! This feast was designated as one of the four Marian feasts, along with the Annunciation, Nativity, and Purification by Pope Sergius I.[20] Why was this particular text selected when it does not even contain the main figure of the feast day? Apparently Mary of Bethany, by sitting at the feet of Jesus, best exemplified Mary, the mother of Jesus, who in the minds of medieval monastic monks, imagined that babies thrive when the mother merely gazes at them adoringly. It has occurred to me that the origin of the disparity in stature between the sisters, Mary being preferred, may have started very early as adoration of the Madonna flourished. Between the sisters, Mary was perceived as the woman most closely imitating the mother of Jesus.

Bernard of Clairvaux, (1090–1153) noted that Christ was the example of living both the active and contemplative life together. He saw both Mary and Martha united in the Blessed Mother Mary. "The 'best part' belongs to

---

15. Quote from Origen, *Frag. 72 of the Hom. On Luke,* in Constable, *Three Studies,* 15.
16. Brauch, *Abusing Scripture,* 153.
17. Constable, *Three Studies,* 15.
18. Bock *Luke Vol.* 2:9:51–24:53, 1041.
19. Schüssler Fiorenza, *But She Said,* 58.
20. Grumett, "Action and/or Contemplation?" 126.

her, who is simultaneously a mother and a virgin."[21] That pretty much rules out any practical application for the rest of us females since.

Meister Eckhart, a mystic and Dominican monk, turned tables in 1300 and preached a famous sermon that praised Martha and criticized Mary.[22] He considered Martha the mature sister who embodied the supreme idea of what a human should be and could become. Meister Eckhart managed to promote Martha to the model for late medieval womanhood. The Protestant tradition did not have such easy exegesis with this passage. Luther paraphrased Jesus' remark as, "Martha, your work must be punished and regarded as worthless . . . I want no work but that of Mary, which is faith." For the Reformers, Martha is the embodiment of righteousness by works. She is trying to earn righteousness, but God makes us righteous by grace. Martha is problematic, useful in practical matters, but less than Mary, and thus "worth-less."[23] Protestants managed to live in peace with Luke 10:38–42 by devising a compromise position: never get obsessive with worldly cares to the point they interfered with service to God.[24] Once the trend was started, other church fathers chimed in. Since it was obviously a women's story, it also reinforced what men wanted to believe about women—they are useful for putting food on the table, but have time left over to listen to us preach.

The most famous work of Teresa of Avila (1515–1582) was inspired by the Vulgate translation of Luke 10, which calls Martha's unnamed village a *castellum*. In *The Interior Castle*, contemplation and action coexist together: "Both Martha and Mary must entertain our Lord and keep Him as their Guest, nor must they be so inhospitable as to offer Him no food. How can Mary do this while she sits at His feet, if her sister does not help her?"[25]

Recent Interpretations

A sampling of modern commentaries shows that the status quo for Mary and Martha has not changed. J.C. Ryle (1816–1900) exemplifies commentators of a few generations ago: "Martha, when Jesus came to her house, rejoiced to see him and busied herself with preparing suitable refreshments.

---

21. Peters, *Many Faces*, 35.

22. Moltmann-Wendel, *The Women*, 28–29.

23. Moltmann-Wendel, *The Women*, 21.

24. Schüssler Fiorenza, *But She Said*, 58.

25. Teresa of Avila, *The Interior Castle*, quoted in Grumett, "Action and/or Contemplation?" 133.

Mary also rejoiced to see him, but her first thought was to sit at his feet and hear his word. Grace reigned in both hearts, but the two women showed the effect of grace in different ways."[26]

Practically all current commentaries set this pericope firmly within a domestic setting of the house of Martha with meal preparation precipitating the ensuing discussion between Martha and Jesus. John Nolland summarizes Luke 10:38–42: "He goes into a particular house . . . Martha's domestic service . . . causes her to be pulled this way and that."[27] Joel Green also finds Luke's narration concerned with hospitality because the opening statement describes travel.[28] "The manner of Martha's hospitality is ill adapted to the sort of hospitality for which Jesus seeks (10:5–12)."[29] Green also finds Mary's "listening" more appropriate than Martha's "doing." Both of these commentaries make special note that "in her house" is a textual variant. Darrell Bock has the scene firmly in the kitchen: "First, we see Martha, busy and harried, engaged in getting everything right for Jesus' visit, and disturbed over Mary's lack of help."[30] Bock does omit "in her house" from his translation and has a long note of explanation. Joseph Fitzmyer is firmly in the domestic camp: "Martha, the perfect hostess, and Mary, the perfect disciple."[31] Howard Marshall continues: "Martha, as the hostess, was distracted from listening by her preparations for a meal."[32] Robert Tannehill translates *diakonia* in this instance as "caring for one's guest, especially through providing a meal."[33]

L.T. Johnson omits "in her house" from his translation and offers no notes of explanation, but his commentary holds to the tradition: "The Prophet is received with hospitality by the two sisters."[34] There is no break in the trend; many commentaries across a wide range of perspectives firmly plant Mary and Martha in their home, receiving Jesus in a meal setting.[35]

26. J.C. Ryle, *Luke*, 147.

27. Nolland, *Luke 9:21–18:34*, 602.

28. Green, *The Gospel*, 433.

29. Green, *The Gospel*, 434.

30. Bock, *Luke Vol. 2:9:51–24:53*, 1037.

31. Fitzmyer, *Gospel According to Luke (X–XXIV)*, 892.

32. Marshall, *Gospel of Luke*, 451.

33. Tannehill, *Luke*, 185.

34. Johnson, *Luke*, 175.

35. Hendriksen, *Luke*, 603; Tiede, *Luke*, 210; Craddock, *Luke*, 152; Ringe, *Luke*, 161–162; Corley, *Private Women*, 137.

Some commentators take special note of the placement of Mary and Martha in conjunction with other lessons concerning discipleship. Bock finds the pericope one of three that concerns the disciple's responsibilities before God. In Luke 10:25–37, the disciple loves the neighbor, followed by Mary who demonstrates love of God, and 11:1–13 teaches prayer.[36]

The most recent commentaries continue the tradition that a balance must be maintained between active and contemplative service, even if stated in ever more creative ways. David Jeffery sees Luke 10:38–42 as purposefully following the Good Samaritan: "Active service of the Lord cannot be long practiced without sitting at the feet of the Lord."[37] Justo Gonzales also sees significance in the juxtaposition of the two passages. He asks: "What would have been Martha's reaction if she had heard the Good Samaritan parable?"[38] David Garland repaints the traditional scene: "Instead of having a private word with Mary or giving her a meaningful look, Martha wipes her dishpan hands on her apron and complains directly to Jesus about her do-nothing sister."[39] The emphasis on Martha's attitude instead of her activity is pointed out by Garland who says: "She (Martha) is scolded not for hustling and bustling but for fretting and fussing."[40] John Carroll is on the right track when he notes: "The distinct roles of the two sisters seem almost a caricature, dividing labors that belong together in the disciple: receiving the Lord's teaching and serving, or hearing and doing."[41] To his credit he notes an important theme that I will pick up: "This juxtaposition of Martha's conventional service of household management with Mary's receptivity to the word of Jesus recalls his own redefinition of family in the company he is gathering around him, composed of all who hear and do God's purpose (8:19–21).[42] He also notes the connection to the following pericope where Jesus teaches prayer.[43]

---

36. Bock, *Luke*, Vol. 2:9:51–24:53, 1038.

37. Jeffrey, *Luke*, 153.

38. "Had Martha been present when Jesus told the parable, and the point of the parable was that one should serve those in need, she would have more than sufficient reason to be angry!" Justo L. Gonzales, *Belief: A Theological Commentary on the Bible, Luke* (Louisville: Westminster John Knox Press, 2010), 141.

39. Garland, *Luke*, 453.

40. Also, "She is in danger of majoring in minors and passing over what is of chief importance." Garland, *Luke*, 455.

41. Carroll, *Luke*, 247.

42. Carroll, *Luke*, 247.

43. Carroll, *Luke*, 248.

A recent monograph by F. Scott Spencer compares Mary and Martha with OT texts that handle the "discordant household" theme, particularly rival women within the same house.[44] He concedes that the Lukan pair do not correspond well with the examples because the OT stories he uses are all stories of women involved with marital or infertility conflicts. In fact, he says Luke is not much interested in maternal roles outside the birth narrative. Luke's interest is in loosening kinship ties, and forming the new household of God.[45] As my thesis progresses, this is a theme that I will develop to a further extent. I also agree with his attempt to emphasize "individual integrity and the mutual solidarity" between the sisters.[46] I certainly agree with this aim, but I project a text with a much more vivid result.

G. B. Caird in 1963 noted: "Few stories in the Gospels have been as consistently mishandled as this one."[47] Craddock summarizes the conundrum: "If we censure Martha too harshly, she may abandon serving altogether, and if we commend Mary too profusely, she may sit there forever."[48] Barbara Reid, whose work I found useful throughout the whole study, notes: "The tensions imbedded in this story raise more questions and interpretive problems than any other Lukan text involving women."[49] Considering the long list of esteemed commentaries on this text, it seems to be bucking an overwhelming trend to get Mary out of the house and Martha away from kitchen duties. This book will pursue this possibility with a closer look at the text.

My Journey to a New Perspective on Mary and Martha

Many of us welcomed Ben Witherington's observation in 1984 when he brought Mary and Martha to popular recognition as useful to grant permission for women to study theology and not limit themselves to domestic occupations.[50] His affirmation of women as legitimate students of the Word was repeated in numerous devotions and sermons. I personally found Mary's permission to study at the feet of Jesus a source of strength at differ-

44. Spencer, *Salty Wives*, 145–189.

45. Spencer, *Salty Wives*, 168.

46. Spencer, *Salty Wives*, 172.

47. Caird, *The Gospel of St. Luke*, 149.

48. Craddock, *Luke*, 152.

49. Reid, *Women in the Gospel of Luke*, 144.

50. Witherington, *Women in the Ministry*, 101.

ent times of my journey when I felt estranged from the church. However, problems remained: the story was rescued to empower women's study at the feet of Jesus, but at the expense of alienating Martha's activity. Also, Mary does not do anything with her learning, i.e., she certainly does not go out and teach others elsewhere. An additional issue is that Jesus is set in opposition to Jewish Rabbis, who were said to not allow women to learn as disciples.

Many creative—and humorous, if they were not so desperate—interpretations of the text suggest ways to lessen Jesus' scolding of Martha and leave room for conditional approval of her activity. Frequent attempts are made to portray Jesus as "lending a hand" and showing more sympathy to the hard-working Martha.[51] Rehabilitations of the text that attempt to portray the sisters more equally fall flat, as well as making the story into something that it is not.[52] No one lacks for an opinion and there certainly is not a consensus on these two ancient ladies who stick in the memory and have drawn controversy for almost two millennia.

Several exegetes have instinctively felt that something is wrong with the inescapable conclusion that Mary's activity of learning at-the-feet is "worth more," and Martha's activity of serving is "worth-less."[53] Many ideas from diverse sources resulted in the *New Perspective on Mary and Martha,* and I would like to set forward my progression of thought as well as give credit to whom credit is due. One of the first sources I read was Elizabeth Schüssler-Fiorenza, who reassessed the pericope in 1992. Her main thesis is that the text reflects issues of the Lukan community many decades later, not those of the time of Jesus. The topic is not about proper hospitality, but the issue of women's leadership.[54] This is a possibility, but more useful to my thesis, she questions the common assumption that Luke 10:38–42 is about hostess duties. Another important point she makes is that the climactic word of Jesus does not mention her responsibilities but reproaches Martha because she is anxious and troubled.[55]

---

51. "I wish I could say that Jesus asked the disciples to do the washing up," quoted from Rosemary King, "Martha and Mary," 459–461.

52. Reid, *Choosing,* 160.

53. Moltmann-Wendel, *The Women,* 21.

54. Schüssler Fiorenza, *But She Said,* 62–68.

55. Schüssler Fiorenza, *But She Said,* 57.

John Collins has written a sizeable book on the possible meanings of the word translated "serving."[56] Yet, he does not agree with Schüssler Fiorenza that the story is about diaconal duties and maintains that the pericope concerns the priority of hearing Jesus. So he ultimately stays in the well-worn camp. I particularly resonated with Barbara Reid who agrees that *diakonia* can refer to all kinds of ministries, official as well as informal.[57] Reid proposes that Martha is upset "about" or "concerning" her ministry and is not being allowed to pursue the ministry for which she is called. While I agree that Martha could be "serving," in many different ways, I will conclude that the specific *diakonia* being performed by Martha is not important, only that she claims to need Mary's help with whatever it is that she is doing. Once Martha is freed from entertaining too many unexpected guests, the story opens up.

Warren Carter goes into the nature of Martha's reception as similar to the accepting of the seventy in the text beginning at 10:1.[58] Martha, as an ideal disciple, "heard" Jesus and accepted God who sent him. Martha's "receiving" of Jesus is primarily the acceptance of his message, whether or not she is accepting him into her house. Dorothy Lee points out the necessity of separating the two pericopes of Luke 10 and John 11–12. Because the Johannine events take place in Bethany near Jerusalem, one does not have to assume that Mary and Martha are located near Jerusalem in Luke.[59] A change of landscape adds a new horizon to the story.

Mary Rose D'Angelo argues for Luke as having a dual apologetic function.[60] The number of stories that feature women is increased for the catechetical instruction and edification of women. At the same time, Luke's portrayal of women is addressed to the detractors, both inside and outside the Christian circle, who see women's increased leadership as a sign of social disorder, and therefore restricts their ability to minister and prophesy. This opens the possibility that what is not written in the text is often as revealing as what is written. To me, this realization opened new windows of understanding that important items lurk beneath the surface of the text. These authors got me started into the study and more will be added as the book progresses.

56. Collins, *Diakonia,*

57. Reid, *Choosing,* 147.

58. Carter, "Getting Martha," 165–166.

59. Lee, *Flesh and Glory,* 198.

60. D' Angelo, "Women in Luke-Acts," 441–61.

2

The Sisters Remain Illusive

HISTORICAL AND CULTURAL BACKGROUND

PUT ON FIRST-CENTURY GLASSES to look into the world of Mary and Martha and remove ourselves from the twenty-first, at least temporarily. Certain cultural questions repeatedly enter conversations about these sisters. The first topic that typically comes up when discussing the Lukan passage includes the acceptability of women as legitimate students of a rabbi. Closely following, in both the Lukan and Johannine passages, male-female relations in an honor-shame society influence interpretation, e.g., the appropriateness of Jesus meeting with women who are not related to him. The topics that pertain to Luke 10:38–42 will be discussed in this chapter. I will visit additional cultural subjects in chapter 5 that pertain to John 11–12 such as foot-washing protocol, women's hairstyles, banquets, and burial.

Were Women Allowed to Study?

Particularly pertinent to our study is Mary and Martha as "sitters at the feet." How unique was it for Jesus to allow Mary as a woman to learn at his feet? What did that look like? It is frequently repeated that Jewish women were forbidden to learn Torah, and that Jesus was blatantly breaking with tradition by allowing Mary to learn at his feet. Rabbi Eliezer is quoted in this context as saying, "If any man gives his daughter knowledge of the

Law it is as though he taught her lechery."[1] Also, "Better to burn the Torah than place it in the mouth of a woman."[2] Several commentators find these quotes to be overstated, misused, and also denigrate first-century Judaism. These sources are from around A.D. 200, and reflect later tradition that may not be the practice at the time of Jesus. In addition, the quotes have been taken out of context.[3]

A conflicting quote from the same period of Ben Azzai states: "A man ought to give his daughter a knowledge of the Law."[4] Another example states a religious duty to educate both sons and daughters.[5] The opinion that in the first century the rabbis generally held a negative view of Torah study for Jewish women has more recently been challenged with more positive evidence that at least some Jewish women studied the Torah.[6] The ideals concerning women that have been handed down from writers such as Josephus may reflect women's place in the world as they would have it, but probably did not resemble the actual experience of women.

There were no binding legal injunctions in Judaism at that time against women engaging in theological studies, although it seems they were also not particularly encouraged.[7] Jesus was also not a traditional rabbi teaching Torah in a formal setting, so any comparisons with the usual experience of Jewish women as learners probably does not apply in the community of his disciples. Stevan Davies observes, "Unless it can be shown that such charismatic individuals normally refused to instruct women, then the portrait drawn in the corpus simply reflects reality as Luke knew it."[8]

Remarkably, throughout his ministry, Jesus never limited those who could benefit from his instruction. He often preached to large multitudes in outdoor locations where everyone could hear him, regardless of sex, age, and nationality (e.g., Mark 6:34). When he taught at the temple, it was in the public courts (e.g., Matt. 26:55), which was an area accessible to any audience. Although the disciples sometimes express surprise and discomfort

---

1. m. Sota 3:4 quoted in Reid, *Choosing*, 152.

2. t. Sota 21b quoted in Reid, *Choosing*, 152.

3. Koperski, "Women and Discipleship in Luke 19:38–42 and Acts 6:1–7," 163–64.

4. m. Sota 3:4 quoted in Reid, *Choosing*, 153.

5. m. Ned. 4:3 quoted in Reid, *Choosing*, 153.

6. Cohick, *Women*, 209. She describes Jewish women interpreting the law with the Essenes at Qumran and other rabbinic evidence of women studying. 195–209.

7. Reid, *Choosing*. 152.

8. S. Davies, "Women in the Third Gospel," 186.

with Jesus when he interacted with women, this was more likely because they were foreign, as were the Samaritan woman in 4:4–42, and the Syrophoenician woman in Mark 7:24–30.

Jesus certainly was a radical master-rabbi-teacher who generously encouraged women disciples to serve him in non-traditional ways. In this narrative, if Mary was present at that moment in this scene learning at his feet, or if Mary and Martha both had a history as students at his feet, it illustrates that he persistently included women in learning situations. In John 11:28, Martha calls Mary to Jesus by saying, "*ho didaskalos* is here." In the Fourth Gospel, "The Teacher" was a natural way of referring to Jesus before the resurrection. It is revealing that this name for Jesus is used between two women, and he is known as "The Teacher" to Mary and Martha.[9]

In this particular episode of Luke as traditionally interpreted, Mary's learning at the feet of Jesus in her private home among fellow Christ-followers, would not have attracted any unusual attention to her as a female learner. Remembering this, if male listeners were in Jesus' presence that day, as the scene is traditionally reenacted, they were not elbowing each other in the ribs if they noted a fellow believer, not a foreigner, but a Jewish sister, among them listening to Jesus' word in her own home.

In conclusion, Mary's, or Martha's listening to Jesus' teaching in the position of a disciple would not be remarkable behavior. Among the Jews, it may have been unusual that a woman took interest in study of the law, but was not explicitly forbidden. In the context of a community of early followers of Jesus, if Mary and/or Martha were learning from him, they were not attracting attention. Jesus had female disciples following him (e.g., Luke 8:1–3), he taught informally in the open air to crowds, and publically taught individual women. While I agree it is extremely vital for women to be totally affirmed as his valid students, in this passage even greater opportunities for women will come forward. As the chapters of this work progress, it will be seen that the pericope in Luke goes far beyond the appropriateness of women learning from Jesus. Luke illustrates what women are doing with that learning and the new dilemmas created by their activities.

All People Knew Their Place!

Deeper understanding of ancient concepts of shame/honor and private/public helps to uncover normal and abnormal behavior in the pericopes

9. Köstenberger, *John*, 337.

under study. Life was governed by struggle for a portion of the limited amount of honor available. These narratives must be read with an eye towards what would be normal or scandalous behavior between men and women in view of first-century expectations. The reader must consistently ask what is right or wrong in the human interactions in this narrative.[10] The view of the Gospel author can be interpreted for signs of support or undermining of social norms.

A man's honor depended on his ability to protect, defend, and look after the sexual exclusivity of women in his family. Protection of her "shame" or purity resulted in customs and roles that restricted her exposure to non-related males.[11] Women's roles in Jewish antiquity required that women did not appear in public places, especially alone, and absent the company of male relatives. They certainly did not speak to non-related males in public.

In both of these texts, Luke 10:38–42 and John 11:1—12:11, Jesus appears to disregard social codes typical in the culture for elite males. An item of protocol is broken in Luke 10:38 when Jesus, an unmarried rabbi, has apparently left his disciples according to the singular verb, and meets Martha and/or Mary unaccompanied. They are not identified as relatives and any man, or servants that may be in the house are unmentioned.[12] By chapter 10, Jesus already has ample history of less than culturally approved contact with women. In Luke alone, at the end of chapter 7 Jesus tolerates, and indeed wholly praises the worship of the unnamed woman who anoints his feet, despite the background protests of the host. At the beginning of chapter 8, Jesus includes female followers with his disciples as they traveled. Honor and shame standards in John 11–12 will be discussed below.

Jesus' behavior, as recorded by both of these Gospel writers, deviated remarkably from the norms of the honor/shame society of the first century. Without attempting to understand the Mediterranean world, many important subtleties would be missed that hint of the uniqueness of the message for both women and men. Jesus was forming a new code of honor by gathering a new community of believers, where expected gender roles and servant status were eased. Family bonds by blood relations were loosened, servant leadership replaced hierarchy, and ministry callings were determined by giftedness, not appearance.

---

10. Neyrey, S.J., *The Gospel of John*, 144.

11. Malina, *The New Testament World*, 47.

12. Esler and Piper, *Lazarus, Mary and Martha*, 49.

A Dinner Invitation?

Placing the traditional understanding of the Lukan scene of 10:38–42 in the dining room has some support in the vocabulary of the text. If Martha received Jesus as an itinerant teacher and long-time friend, dining of some kind was probably forthcoming. Luke's word choice of *merida* (10:42) can have a double meaning and hints of a meal context.[13] Also, of all the Gospels, Luke particularly favors meal settings to present important teachings of Jesus (7:36–50, 11:37–54, 14:1–24, 15:1–32).[14]

But, setting Luke 10:38–42 into a dining situation in many ways obfuscates more important messages and diverges down some irrelevant "rabbit paths." Furthermore, as logical and familiar as it seems that other guests, including disciples, would be present in a meal setting, the Lukan text simply does not specify a meal taking place, or the presence of anyone other than Jesus and Martha. Dining customs will be revisited in the Johannine study.

Jesus Did Not Mind His Manners

To understand these texts, the reader must expect differences between the first-century world of Greco-Roman culture and the modern reader. In addition, the amount of assimilation of Gentile customs into a Jewish household is difficult to determine. The payoff in thoroughly knowing the norms of the prevailing culture and the Jewish culture of our subjects, is the realization that where the narratives indicate actions outside the norm for that culture, it is a point of importance in the teaching of Jesus. The many ways in which Jesus breaks with traditional societal roles reveals his bigger purposes in forming the new community of believers.

WHERE IS BETHANY?

In the midst of this study of the sisters of Bethany, I discovered unexpected enlightenment in a tourist gift shop while I was traveling around the Sea of Galilee. I casually purchased a book by Bargil Pixner: *With Jesus Through Galilee According to the Fifth Gospel*. This book opened up the possibility

---

13. Nolland, *Luke*, 604. In 10:42b τὴν ἀγαθὴν μερίδα could be translated as "Mary has chosen the better portion of a meal." Μερίδα was used in the LXX for food portions.

14. Blomberg, *Contagious*, 130.

that the so-called sisters of Bethany in Luke 10 were not yet associated with the village of Bethany near Jerusalem. It is puzzling that Luke 10:38 does not mention a location for his Mary and Martha story. If it logically fits in with Jesus' movements during the Galilean mission according to Luke, then the location would be in northern Galilee, not near Jerusalem as also noted by Lee.[15] Many commentaries note that at this point Jesus would more likely be in Samaria or Galilee.[16] Agreed, it is a difficult adjustment to think of the Lukan pericope as taking place in another location; however, there really is no reason to place the conversation between Jesus and Martha near Jerusalem, where the beloved story has been placed for so long in the imagination.

Several locales are tantalizingly unspecified in Jesus' early ministry as in Mark 10:1, "Jesus went into the region of Judea and across the Jordan." Ten verses later, a conversation takes place in a specific house: "When they were in the house again, the disciples asked Jesus about this." What house could this be? Again, in John 1:37–39, John and two of his disciples ask, "Where are you staying?" Jesus answers, "Come and you will see." He may have been staying with relatives in Kochaba.[17] This location is in Batanea, otherwise known in the Bible as Bashan, or today's Golan Heights northeast of the Sea of Galilee. Jesus is said to leave from this northern located Bethany for Galilee in John 1:43. Then he calls Phillip who was from Bethsaida on the north shore of the Sea of Galilee, which he reached within one day of travel, presumably by foot.

Perhaps he was staying at, or near a property of Mary and Martha, or with relatives. My premise does not depend on the accuracy of this background on Mary and Martha's family, but it coincides with other traditions of an important family: their mother came from a royal line of Israel, and their father was a Syrian named Titeophilus, a chief satrap of the province.[18]

15. Lee, *Flesh and Glory,* 198.

16. Esler and Piper, *Lazarus,* 49.

17. Bargil Pixner O.S.B., *With Jesus through Galilee According to the Fifth Gospel* (Rosh Pina: Corazin, 1992), 18. Eusebius A.D. 263–339 quotes Julius Africanus of Emmaus who wrote about AD 200 that relatives of the family of Jesus had kept genealogies to preserve the proof of their Davidic ancestry. They originated from the Jewish villages of Nazara (Nazareth) and Cochaba (Kochaba) in Batanea (or Bashan), a Jewish settlement to the east of the Sea of Galilee.

18. Peters, *Many Faces,* 195. From the *Pseudo-Marcilia* text, based on the version found in the Bibliotheca Hagiographica Latina 5546a as published in *Boninus Mombritis, Sanctuarius, seu Vitae Sanctorum, Mediolani*: ante 1480. They possessed by hereditary right a great patrimony and also many lands and slaves and much money. Property

This report dates from 1480 and the earlier sources are unknown, but if any shred of evidence is valid, they were from a wealthy and influential family, perhaps with a Syrian connection.

If Mary and Martha had a home northeast of the Sea of Galilee, the event which Luke 10:38–42 alone records, occurs not in Bethany near Jerusalem, but northeast of Galilee in Batanea. Moving briefly into John 11–12 to the raising of Lazarus and Mary's anointing, perhaps some short period of time before Mary and Martha receive word that their brother in Bethany near Jerusalem is ill, they were at their home in Batanea. Jesus was with them or with relatives in the area. Mary and Martha make the trip back to Jerusalem, find that Lazarus is close to death, and then send back a messenger for Jesus to come. This would explain how they knew of Jesus' location when they sent him the message, "Lord, the one you love is sick" (John 11:3). They also knew when to expect him to arrive, because they knew the time necessary to travel the distance and were very aware that he was overdue for arrival, adding to the disappointment when Lazarus was already dead.[19]

One more puzzling remark may be explained if Luke 10:38–42 takes place in their permanent home, and Bethany near Jerusalem is a temporary residence while their brother is ill. In John 11:34, Jesus asks, "Where have you laid him?" which sounds like Jesus was not familiar with the small village where the location of burial sites would be well known. Perhaps the occasion of Lazarus' revivification was the first time Jesus was in Bethany near Jerusalem, and maybe he also didn't know where the sisters were housed when he paused on the road.

The Essenes established and maintained an extensive system of facilities for the poor and sick.[20] Bethany is mentioned in the Dead Sea Scrolls (11 Q Temple 46:16–18) as the home to one of the leper colonies of that day. This scroll documents the necessity of establishing three locations east of Jerusalem for the care of pilgrims afflicted with illness that rendered them ritually unclean. Capper notes the possibility that Lazarus traveled

---

attributed to them included Bethany and most of Jerusalem.

19. Further evidence for a location of Bethany across the Jordan in Batanea: Pharisees were apparently active in this area where otherwise the influence of the Essenes was strongest. The two schools had different views about marriage, therefore the discussion on marriage in Mk 10:1–9. "Therefore what God has joined together, let man not put asunder."

20. Capper, "Essene Community Houses," 496.

to Bethany for treatment of his unnamed illness that eventually was fatal.[21] The anointing stories of Mark 14:3–9 and Matthew 26:6–13 take place in Bethany at the house of Simon the Leper. Judas' remark at Mary's use of expensive ointment in John 12:5 would make sense in the context that Bethany was home to a leper colony, and reflects close contact with a population of needy people.

The geographical theory for the Lukan scene taking place in Batanea is not essential to backing this element of the thesis because the sisters' involvement in Jesus' early evangelistic travels could be based in Bethany by Jerusalem as well. However, placing Mary and Martha in a home northeast of Galilee explains details concerning the contact between them and Jesus in John 11. If Mary and Martha were residing in the area of Jesus' early activity, it would give them opportunity to be converted to the Jesus movement at the same time as the twelve disciples were being assembled and lengthens the time of their friendship with Jesus (Luke 8:1–3). To add to the confusion, two locations named Bethany are mentioned in the Gospel of John. First, in 1:28 is mention of "Bethany on the other side of the Jordan where John was baptizing," which is probably a region called Batanea and not a specific village. Second, there is the village of Bethany near Jerusalem in 11:1 where the Lazarus events take place. More will be divulged in the upcoming chapters concerning the importance of this more accurate location of Luke 10:38–42.

At this point, I will also insert further information on the historical Mary, Martha, and Lazarus, also known by the Hebrew form of his name, Eleazar. Frederick W. Balz has researched the Talmud, Midrashim, and the list of priests compiled by Josephus.[22] He claims evidence for the three siblings being children of Boethus a high priest, and that Eleazar (Lazarus) was also a high priest for a short time. Balz also proposes that Simon the Leper was a younger brother in the family. He is a strong proponent of Lazarus being the "beloved disciple" in John, who being close to the family of the high priest, would explain his ability to enter the house of Caiaphas on the night of Jesus' trial without opposition(John 18:15). I am including this extra-biblical background as something to keep in mind throughout reading this book; whether or not Mary and Martha were daughters and sisters of high priests, is not essential to my premises. And yet, if the

---

21. Capper, "Essene Community Houses," 497.
22. Baltz, *Lazarus*, 73 ff.

above information is plausible, it would indeed be safe to assume they were not short of resources, and the evidence is greater that they were very well-known.

I am going to continue my new perspective on Mary and Martha assuming that their original and permanent residence was not at Bethany near Jerusalem. Luke 10:38–42 takes place in Galilee or northeast of the Sea of Galilee. The events of John 11–12 take place in the village of Bethany near Jerusalem. Lazarus moved to Bethany when he fell ill for treatment of his illness, or possibly he already resided in Jerusalem when his health failed. Mary and Martha came when they learned of the severity of his illness or that he was near death. They then took up residence in a house that was known as the house of Simon the Leper just over the hill from Jerusalem.

3

The Greek Foundations

LUKE 10:38–42 IS TYPICALLY cited to illustrate the prioritizing of activities and making time for study of the word. Traditional interpretations—which have been repeated for generations without serious re-evaluation—result in many unsolved quandaries. Mary is commended by Jesus for making study most important, and Martha is mildly rebuked for being "too busy." Yet Jesus in 10:5–7 extols hospitality, especially to traveling disciples, and sets himself as the example of being a servant (e.g., Lk 22:27). It seems incongruous in the context that Jesus would not welcome Martha's service as exemplary. In no other text of Luke-Acts is "service" *diakonia* assessed negatively.[1] Luke describes discipleship as both "hearing and doing" the word in 6:47, 8:15, 8:21, and 11:28.

The reader of Luke could rightly expect that Jesus would use this situation with Mary and Martha to continue the themes he has been teaching in previous chapters, such as servanthood, putting others before self, and the value of hospitality. Yet Jesus seems to be teaching at cross-purposes to prior chapters of Luke, and does not appear to uphold many values of hospitality that ancient as well as contemporary readers hold dear. Perhaps the dissonance between Jesus' words in Luke 10:38–42, and his prior teaching is unfounded because I will examine the details with the result that this pericope will have a completely different emphasis.

We noted above that this passage has required at least yearly attention because of its place in the lectionary on the Assumption of Mary. Perhaps because of that August date in the middle of a hot month, countless priests

---

1. Hentschel, *Diakonia im Neuen Testament,* 238.

and pastors over all those centuries struggled with the text. They were overcome by heat, and decided to pull out the homily from the year before. Why did no one really look at the text creatively? I hesitantly suggest that because the main characters are women, their imaginations were somewhat constricted by preconceptions of how women think. Of course Mary and Martha had to be bickering over kitchen work. What else do women do?

In this chapter, I am presenting the nitty-gritty of the Greek basis of my perspective on Mary and Martha. New insights into the grammar, vocabulary, and textual variants are the foundation of this new perspective, and very essential to understanding how I reached my conclusions. However, for those readers who must by-pass the Greek, I will concentrate the Greek exegesis in the first half of the chapter, and the conclusion of this chapter will summarize my findings in plain English.

THE GREEK OF LUKE

At the beginning of Luke 10:38, Jesus is traveling with an unidentified plural group that is grammatically masculine, but could be used inclusively to include females. This group is traveling and come to κώμην τινά "a certain village" which is inexplicably unnamed. By 10:38b, the subject pronoun with the verb is suddenly singular αὐτὸς εἰσῆλθεν "he entered." A certain woman named Martha receives αὐτόν "him," which is again singular. The rest of the traveling group has literarily, if not literally, disappeared.

Luke also does not describe the exact setting where Martha greets Jesus, whether it is her house, on a road, public or private. The words "into her house" are included in the TNIV, KJV, and NASB translations. Luke 10:38–42 has a high number of textual variants, which indicates difficulty with interpretation from the first centuries. Textual evidence for αὐτόν εἰς τὴν οἰκίαν, "him into the house," in the manuscripts is mixed. The UBS stops with ὑπεδέξατο αὐτόν, "she received him." This reading is supported in the earliest parchments, where αὐτόν, "him," stands alone in p45, p75 and B. Another variant adds a possessive genitive "her," αὐτόν εἰς τὴν οἰκίαν αὐτῆς, "him into her house." Several commentaries note the omission of "house," but still go on to include it in the translation. Nolland includes the phrase and notes, "The full phrase could be a scribal completion, but is probably original as part of the terms that evoke the mission materials of Luke 9:1–6."[2] Green also includes the phrase in his translation and admits

---

2. Nolland, *Luke*, 600.

it is omitted in the early parchments. He says: "Even if, as seems probable, variant forms were introduced to draw out the meaning of ὑπεδέξατο αὐτόν, 'she received him,' this phrase is already implicit in the Lukan use of "to welcome" or "to extend hospitality."[3] Bock does not include it in his translation, but he sees a domestic scene in a house "vividly."[4] He notes: "that many manuscripts include the longer phrase in different forms, speaks against either of the longer options being original. The reading chosen does not affect the general meaning, only its specificity." Bock goes on to say he prefers the shorter reading.[5] The conclusion from this discussion is that the earliest parchment, p75, from the early third century, omits mention of a house, and it is the shortest reading. Therefore, as I am pursuing the new perspective on Mary and Mary, the phrase including the reference to a house is omitted.

The nature of Martha's reception of Jesus warrants exploration. Luke starts the action between Martha and Jesus with ὑπεδέξατο αὐτόν, "she received him," which generally means to offer hospitality as a guest, but can also mean to simply "to receive someone."[6] Other Lukan uses of the verb include the same phrase in Luke 19:6 where Jesus looks up in the tree to see Zacchaeus and says, "I must stay in your house today." In this case, it is very clear that the reception involved staying at a house. The text in Acts 17:7 also clearly includes Jason's house. The root verb δέχομαι, "receive," can indicate approval or conviction by accepting, and is used similarly in 8:13: "Those on the rock are the ones who receive the word with joy when they hear it." This sense also occurs in 9:53, 10:8 and 10:10 where Jesus poses two possible scenarios to "the seventy" upon entering a town (10:7): they may or may not be welcomed. In 9:53, Jesus was not "welcomed" (ἐδέξαντο) by the Samaritans because he was headed to Jerusalem. Therefore, the δέχομαι-related verbs can indicate acceptance of Jesus and his mission. Pauline examples are found in Romans 16:1, where Phoebe is to be "received" (προσδέχομαι), and in Philippians 2:25, Epaphroditus is to be "received" (προσδέχομαι). The conclusion is that if "house" is not included in the oldest texts, then ὑπεδέξατο can be a more general "welcome" or better, "received" as in Martha received Jesus and his message by becoming a disciple.

3. Green, *The Gospel*, 433.
4. Bock, *Luke*, 1039.
5. Bock, *Luke*, 1043.
6. Bauer, et al. *A Greek-English Lexicon*, 1037, abbreviated BDAG hereafter.

Luke 10:39 continues, "And this one (fem.) has a sister called Mary." The conjunction καὶ to the next phrase, is often not translated, as in the NIV: "She had a sister called Mary, who sat at the Lord's feet . . ." Καὶ can be translated "and, but" or "also." If it is translated as "also," then both Mary and Martha are equally identified as disciples.[7] "Who" (ἥ) is inserted in a widely dispersed set of manuscripts. The ἥ "who" is omitted by p45, p75, ℵ, and L, it is found in A, B, C, D, W, Θ, Ψ. This geographic distribution speaks for its originality; its presence indicates that the first use of καὶ should be translated "also."[8] By translating the καὶ as "also," and using one important variant, the transition is completed as: "And this woman has a sister called Mary, who also sat herself at the feet." With this relative pronoun ἥ as the subject, the participle παρακαθεσθεῖσα, can be read substantively, "a person who sits oneself." Παρακαθεσθεῖσα is in the middle voice and can indicate that Mary (and Martha) took the initiative in setting themselves beside Jesus as disciples.

The KJV reads, "And she had a sister called Mary, *which also* sat at Jesus' feet, and heard his word." In this case, the translators of the KJV must have noticed a καὶ in whatever Greek source they were working from, and accurately translated it as "also," which is clearly in the UBS text, but has been dropped in most modern English translations. This passage could be describing Mary as also being "a sitter" at the feet of Jesus, in the same manner as Martha. An additional grammatical point is that Luke chose a rarer verb tense, the imperfect, ἤκουεν "was listening," which indicates that the sisters have been hearing the words of Jesus over a period of time.

"But Martha was distracted" (10:40). What kind of service is distracting Martha? The imperfect phrase περιεσπᾶτο περὶ πολλὴν literally means, "was constantly being pulled concerning much." Περιεσπάω is a NT *hapax legomenon* and indicates "being pulled away" by something and can refer not only to distraction and busyness, but also to being overburdened.[9] The Greek imperfect tense indicates that this was not a one-time event, but occurred frequently over a period of time. The narrator uses the verb to state an objective fact; Martha was worried and it was not neurotic obsessiveness on her part.[10] Interestingly, a closely related word, ἀπερισπάστως, is used in 1 Cor. 7:35, a passage that some feel Paul may have written with an oral ver-

---

7. D'Angelo, "Women," 454–55.

8. Bock, *Luke*, 1043.

9. BDAG, 804.

10. Johnson, *Luke*, 173.

sion of the Mary and Martha story in mind.[11] Although this scene is usually imagined as a one-time situation on this particular occasion and day, Luke's choice of verb here indicates that Martha's state of being overwhelmed was an on-going issue with her.

Discourse on *diakonia*

What was the cause of Martha's distraction? Before we smell wonderful cooking fragrances wafting through Martha's house, reconsider the possible "service" Martha was offering. The Greek text uses only one word *diakonia* which is familiar because, in most translations, when it refers to work done by a man, it is translated as "deacon or minister."[12] Extensive study has been done on the meaning of *diakonia* starting with J.N. Collins in 1990, who worked from classical Greek texts to expand the semantic field of *diakonia* from lowly house service "to be a go-between or emissary," such as an ambassador or curior.[13] The Jewish understanding of "service" has always been assumed, but Collins raised the possibility that NT writers may have also taken *diakonia* in the classic Greek sense of one who is a messenger, spokesperson or agent.[14] Of the thirty-four uses in the NT, fourteen times it is translated as "ministry."[15] It can mean many different kinds of service on the behalf of another, including but not necessarily restricted to serving a meal.[16] Warren Carter makes a convincing argument that Martha is distracted by her responsibilities of leadership and house ministry.[17] In contrast, Tannehill maintains that *diakonia* in this setting refers to hospitality, especially through providing a meal. He does not broaden to the possibility of an established ministry of preaching and leadership.[18] More recently in 2007, Anni Hentschel continues the work on *diakonia* and notes

---

11. For a more complete discussion of the similarity between Luke 10:38–42 and 1 Cor. 7:32–35, see Veronica Koperski, "Women and Discipleship," 165–166.

12. Romans 16:1: "I commend to you our sister Phoebe, a servant (*diakonon*) of the church." When the word refers to a woman it is translated to "servant" although the TNIV footnotes it.

13. Collins, *Diakonia*.

14. Dunderberg, "Vermittlung," 175–76.

15. Kohlenberger III, *The Greek English Concordance*, 154.

16. Reid, *Choosing the Better Part?* 147.

17. Carter, "Getting Martha," 223.

18. Tannehill, *Luke*, 185.

that the subject can be a man or woman, and indicates ministry in hospitality or in the broader sense, Phoebe being an example in Romans 16:1.[19] She concludes that the understanding of *diakonia* in Luke 10:38–42 is determined by context.[20] She does not find such a strong contrast as Collins, i.e., one meaning does not necessarily preempt the other. Bringing food to the table, or serving in the community in a more official capacity, are not so different.[21]

Acts 6:1–6 illustrates the range of meanings for *diakonia*. Seven Hellenists are appointed to devote themselves to *diakonia* "service at the table" so the apostles could be free to do *diakonia* "service of the word." It is revealing that no further record exists that they ever actually practiced service at the table. At least two in this group, Phillip and Stephen, practiced word-service and became preachers of the early Christian church.[22]

Schüssler Fiorenza states that *diakonia* had already become a technical term for ecclesial leadership in the time that Luke was writing when house-churches provided both preaching of the word and the eucharistic meal celebration.[23] Overall, there is enough evidence that Martha's activity does not have to be restricted to a narrow definition of service. She may very well be a leader of an assembly place for early followers of Christ, instead of, or in addition to, providing as hostess the comforts of a temporary home for Jesus. Later, several well-known women will open their houses and lead churches as Tabitha (Acts 9:36–42), Mary, mother of John Mark (Acts 12:12), and Lydia (Acts 16:15–40).

Continuing the Greek Text

Keeping in mind all of her possible cares, she "appears" (ἐφίστημι) to Jesus and asks him to prevail upon Mary to give her a hand with her διακονία. The use of ἐφίστημι may indicate a lapse of time and change of location from Martha's initial greeting of Jesus. In previous occurrences of the verb in Luke-Acts, it often describes an encounter with divine presence, e.g., 2:9

---

19. Hentschel, *Diakonia*, 436.

20. Hentschel, *Diakonia*, 257

21. Hentschel, *Diakonia*, 239.

22. Schüssler Fiorenza, *But She Said*, 65.

23. Schüssler Fiorenza, *But She Said*, 64.

the angel "appeared" in Bethlehem to the shepherds, as just one of eighteen examples.[24]

The word καταλείπω means "to leave without help"[25] but another meaning is "to depart from a place with implication of finality."[26] Several variants replace the aorist κατέλιπεν for the imperfect κατέλειπεν.[27] If the imperfect verb is considered, then Mary has regularly deserted Martha over a period of time. Καταλείπω is also used in Acts 6 where the apostles do not wish to "leave" the "ministry of the word" (διακονία τοῦ λόγου) in order to wait on tables (διακονέω).[28] The addition of the word μόνην also adds to the sense that the distance between the sisters is more than a few steps between the kitchen and the dining room. She pleads with Jesus to speak to her sister that she will come back to "take hold with" (συναντιλάβηται).[29]

The vocabulary used by Luke indicates that Martha had obligations that reached beyond her duties as hostess on that day. The term for "worried," (μεριμνᾶς), "to be apprehensive, be anxious, be unduly concerned," is used in other NT passages to refer to worldly entanglements as in Jesus' words, "Do not worry about your life, what you will eat or drink," (Matt 6:25–34).[30] Also Jesus says in Luke 12:25–26, "Who of you by worrying can add a single hour to your life? Since you cannot do this very little thing, why do you worry about the rest?" Paul uses the word positively in I Corinthians 7:32–34 where an unmarried woman is μεριμνᾶς "anxious" about the things of the Lord.

In addition, the second adjective for being "upset," (θορυβάζη), is a *hapax legomenon* in the NT. Cognates θορυβέω and θόρυβος are used eleven times and refer to the disturbance of a crowd of people. The first meaning is "disorder of a city close to riot;"[31] the second meaning is "to cause emotional disturbance, disturb, or agitate."[32]

"But only one thing is needed. Mary has chosen what is better, and it will not be taken away from her"(10:43). What exactly is Jesus' intervention

24. Kohlenberger III, *Concordance*, 328.

25. BDAG, 521 §6b.

26. BDAG, 520 §2.

27. A B C L Θ Ξ Nolland, *Luke,* 600, n. i.

28. Corley, *Private Women,* 136.

29. BDAG, 965.

30. BDAG, 632 §1.

31. BDAG, 458 §1.

32. BDAG, 458 §2.

and what is "the good portion" (τὴν ἀγαθὴν μερίδα) that meets Jesus' approval? Jesus' reply to Martha is essentially the climatic teaching, yet his answer is puzzling and has been interpreted many ways. This verse is filled with textual discrepancies, a sure clue that tampering has taken place over the centuries by scribes and commentators who found the verses difficult to understand.[33]

The translations include: "but only one thing is needed" (RSV, KJV) or "but only a few things are necessary, really only one" (NIV, NASB, JB). The former version requires a spiritualized sense as in 18:22: "You lack one thing. Sell everything . . .Then come, follow me."[34] The latter variant is advocated by proponents of the scenario that Jesus is recommending that Martha simplify her meal preparations by saying one dish or maybe a few is all that is necessary.[35] As we have already established, it is not at all clear that the conversation is about meal preparation. A viable translation advocated for this new look for Mary and Martha is: "But one thing is necessary. For Mary has chosen good, and it will not be taken away from her." Τὴν ἀγαθὴν μερίδα "the good portion" does not have to be taken superlatively to mean that Mary chose the "best portion," but can also be translated comparitively, meaning she chose "a good thing." It is notable that Luke uses ἀγαθος rather than καλος which indicates a moral dimension to her choice.[36] Ἀγαθος in Luke-Acts can refer to many different kinds of "good" as gifts, a person's character, and good works (11:13, 23:50, and Acts 9:39).[37] Caring for physical needs is pronounced as "good" by Luke as well as "hearing the word."

CONCLUSIONS OF GREEK STUDY IN PLAIN ENGLISH

Concluding this study of the Greek USB text including variants, here is my proposed translation for this passage:

Luke 10:38–42

38) As they were on their way, he came to a village where a woman named Martha received him.

---

33. Corley, *Private Women*, 138.
34. Marshall, *The Gospel of Luke*, 454.
35. Fee, "One Thing is Needful?" 61–75.
36. Johnson, *Luke*, 174 n 42.
37. Hutson, "Martha's Choice," 139–150.

39) She had a sister called Mary, who also was one who sat at the Lord's feet, always listening to his words.

40) But Martha was constantly torn apart concerning much ministry. She suddenly approached him and said, "Lord, do you not care that my sister regularly leaves me to minister alone? Tell her therefore that she may give me a hand."

41) But the Lord answered her saying, "Martha, Martha, you are anxious and agitated concerning much,

42) but only one thing is needed: For Mary has chosen good and it will not be taken away from her.

At Luke 10:30, Jesus and his entourage are underway as the Lukan travel narrative progresses, but the "certain village" where they are located is unknown. The grammar indicates that Jesus is alone when he meets Martha; his travel companions have somehow disappeared. Whether or not his arrival in this village was the complete surprise often portrayed, Luke himself gives no indication that Martha was overwhelmed serving Jesus and all his disciples. Although it makes a good story, as Luke writes the scene some thirty years later, if Jesus has traveling companions upon meeting Martha, Luke does not consider them essential. This leaves Martha and Jesus alone in the spotlight.

The many textual variants in this passage indicate that scribes considered the text problematic very early after Luke first penned it. "Into the (or her) house," are not included in the earliest texts. Remarkable is the tenacity, despite the questionable textual evidence, with which a domestic location for this scene hangs on. It seems that if the main characters are women, then the temptation to add a house is hard to resist.

Martha's greeting is an illustration of a favorable reception as opposed to those who do not receive Jesus in Luke 10:10.[38] Beyond food and housing, the most vital aspect of "receiving" is the acceptance of the mission and call of Jesus, which Martha and Mary both exemplify.[39] When Jesus sent out "the seventy," he advised, "When you enter a town and are welcomed, eat what is set before you" (Luke 10:7). Jesus surely set the example and followed his own advice. Martha's "receiving" of Jesus in faith was more likely in line with Jesus' modest expectations rather than elaborate preparations often imagined in recreations of this scene. He would be a gracious guest

38. Schüssler Fiorenza, *But She Said,* 66.
39. Carter, "Getting Martha out of the Kitchen" 165–166.

by accepting modest accommodations, and was much less concerned about elaborate hospitality than being received, as in the words of Martha in John 11:27, "the Christ, the Son of God, the one coming into the world." Martha and Mary, having a history as Jesus' disciples and friends, must have been aware of his first preference of being received in faith, followed by simple hospitality. It is doubtful that Martha was "going overboard" with preparations even if this scene is imagined with domestic service in mind. To summarize the findings so far: if "house" is validly omitted, then "received" opens to a deeper meaning and the whole pericope starts to look different. Jesus may or may not be staying at Martha's house; he may or may not be eating her food; but her duties as a hostess are not driving the action.

Verse 39 presents a number of variants and grammatical issues which, when considered in combination, may recover the ancient, original meaning. The more familiar translation describes Mary as presently sitting herself at the feet of Jesus; but, the participle could also name her as "one who sits." "Sitting at the feet" is an idiomatic way of saying that a person is a disciple.[40] In Luke 8:35, the Gerasene man, after being exorcised of many demons, sits at Jesus' feet although the text does not mention that he is listening. In Acts 22:3, Paul trained "at the feet of Gamaliel." D'Angelo agrees with this interpretation and notes, "Once it is recognized that sitting at Jesus' feet and hearing his word indicates discipleship, the meaning should be clear: Martha who received Jesus has a sister who, like Martha herself, was a disciple."[41]

In summary, Luke 10:39 has been traditionally translated to indicate that Mary is, at that moment, sitting at the feet of Jesus. My reading is that both women are reputed to be disciples of Jesus. The reader can safely assume that by this particular scene, both Martha and Mary have already enjoyed a deep relationship with Jesus and have learned much "at his feet." One cannot generalize from these data that Mary is the "studied" sister and Martha the "practical" sister. They have both studied and continue to study.

Luke 8:1–3 describes several women who traveled with Jesus from one town to another, proclaiming the "good news." It is clear that Jesus had female disciples who regularly followed him, but he also had disciples who stayed in their homes and received him there to hear his message. Not all of Jesus' followers were required to leave behind family and homes and follow him, but many did follow him wherever he led, and the families they

---

40. Witherington III, *Women*, 101.

41. D'Angelo, "Women," 454.

left behind also sacrificed. Mary and Martha were Jesus' disciples in every sense of the word.

Essential to the premise of this book is the realization that the main point of this pericope is not Martha's duties as hostess. When Jesus and Martha meet, the possibility that the setting includes a glass of wine, some olives, and a pillow for Jesus is not necessarily ruled out, but does not dominate the scene.

No more information is given about the occasion of Martha's question, "Do you not care that my sister regularly leaves me to serve alone" (author's translation)? Left unsaid in most translations is the deeper meaning of "left alone." She has skipped town, not just stepping into another room, and the imperfect verb tense indicates this is a regular occurance. "Tell her therefore, that she can give me a hand," is the continuation of Martha's speech. The content of what Martha wants Jesus to tell Mary is undisclosed. It is important to note that Martha brought up her difficulty with Mary, not Jesus. He seems to be just fine with the situation between the sisters as it stands.

Jesus' response fits a pattern: whenever anyone asks him to step in to help in a dispute, he resists taking the side of the one asking for help. Other examples of people asking Jesus to intervene include Luke 12:13, "Someone in the crowd said to him, 'Teacher, tell my brother to divide the inheritance with me,'" and John 8:4, "Teacher, this woman was caught in the act of adultery . . . now, what do you say?" In these instances also, Jesus refrains from seeing the dispute with the same eyes as the complainant. Jesus does not respond the way we humans would often wish. On yet another occasion Jesus was confronted with the rhetorical question, "Do you not care?" as Martha did on this day. In Mark 4:38 the disciples wake Jesus in the boat on the Sea of Galilee and ask him, "Do you not care that we drown?" Of course Jesus is aware of a problem, but he wants the disciples to bring it up. Perhaps that is the case with Martha.

Jesus shows deep emotion and concern when he answers with the double vocative, "Martha, Martha." Jesus knew Martha better than Martha knew herself and identified her real problem. It was not that her sister had left her alone to cover all her many responsibilities, but her worry. In other passages of Luke, Jesus has similarly repeated a name twice as in "Jerusalem, Jerusalem," (13:34), and "Simon, Simon," (22:31).[42] Similar to these

---

42. See Luke 6:46, "Why do you call me Lord, Lord," Acts 9:4, Acts 22:7, Acts 26:14, "Saul, Saul."

examples, Jesus is not reprimanding Martha harshly but he intervenes to calm her and turn the situation around.

Jesus uses good psychology when he acknowledges Martha's distress by affirming her feelings, "You are worried and upset about many things." Martha could be seen as "pulled in many directions" by whatever obligations and concerns she had as a leader of an early community of Christ-followers. For purposes of my premise, a broader understanding of Martha's *diakonia* is helpful, as has been documented above, but as the situation is developed, she likely is involved with some combination of ministries.

Imagine also, that Martha could also have heavy family responsibilities. Her sister Mary does not seem to be available to take responsibility for the local demands, or Martha could already be caring for the sick brother introduced in John 11:1. Since no parents are mentioned, the responsibility of caring for elderly parents until their death could have recently fallen on Martha, or perhaps she was widowed with the associated mourning and cares. Whatever her life history, she appears to carry multiple responsibilities.

Overriding all of the earthly responsibilities, both Martha and Mary no doubt sensed that opposition to Jesus was coming to a head and his life was in danger. They would have known about the beheading of John the Baptist, and now Herod is asking about Jesus in 9:9. Jesus himself in 9:22 says that "The Son of Man must suffer many things . . . and he must be killed and on the third day be raised to life." By this point in Luke, Jesus has already resolutely set himself toward Jerusalem (9:51). These scenarios are admittedly conjecture, but so too is the speculation that she was overwhelmed by preparing food for unexpected guests. Martha is enduring a considerable and long-term state of emotional stress caused by many responsibilities. These worries are stronger than just being temporarily overwhelmed with duties as a hostess. However one reads it, Martha was a woman with many demands made upon her!

At this point, it is interesting to note who is getting the most attention grammatically. Traditionally, the story is understood to concern two equal sisters, one who will be eventually vindicated and the other censored. Yet grammatically the sisters are not equal; Martha is the subject of three verbs and one participle, which is even more grammatical attention than Jesus receives. The two verbs that Mary receives in verse 39 are subordinate to "she had a sister."[43]

43. Alexander, "Sister," 206.

Here is the place to pause with recognition of several new pieces of information. Martha receives the most grammatical attention, imperfect verbs are used indicating ongoing action, the vocabulary that describes Martha's inner turmoil is strong, and no hint of the source of this turmoil is given. The description of Martha's worry is stated in language more appropriate to literal desertion than simply being in the next room.

Pulling this all together, it is not Martha's *diakonia* (service) with which Jesus has concern, but her being "worried and upset about much." In addition, very possibly Martha felt a bigger issue looming on the horizen. Similar to Mark 14:7 and John 12:8, Jesus is saying, "Pay attention to me while I am here. Let the future take care of itself." One way of practicing his word is manifested in how disciples handle stress and worry. The next chapter in Luke is on prayer; there may be a connection.

An ongoing question often asked is the reason for Mary's silence. Why is she not given any speech? Why doesn't Martha simply ask her for help? Why doesn't Jesus ask her to help her sister? The conclusion for this new perspective is that Mary does not speak because she is not there. Whether this scene is taking place in a house, a road, a courtyard, or anywhere else, she is not on the premises, she is not within earshot of the conversation. She is not where Martha is; not just removed to another room. She is gone!

Mary has physically left Martha and perhaps frequently leaves to pursue her own *diakonia*. She is involved in some discipleship that does not involve Martha, who is obliged for an undisclosed reason, to stay in the village for her own unspecified *diakonia*. Martha assumes that Jesus knows where Mary is, because she asks Jesus, "Tell her therefore, that she may help me" (10:40b). This would account for Martha's ongoing and acute sense of distress, which in Greek seems greater than if her sister had just left her alone in the kitchen. She pleads with Jesus to speak to her sister that she will come back to "give her a hand." The only other occurrence of this verb is in Romans 8: 26, "The Spirit helps us in our weakness." Martha wants Jesus to ask Mary to come back to their home or village to take on some of the *diakonia* burden for which Martha is responsible, or at least that is her pretense. Is it possible that Martha just wants Mary home? Of course Jesus knows this truth about Martha.

Maybe Mary is following Jesus as a traveling disciple. In Luke 8:1–3, Jesus is noted to be traveling with the twelve as well as "some women." This scene is followed by the sending of "the seventy" in Luke 10:1 both of which closely precede the Luke 10:38–42 passage under discussion. Perhaps Mary has left Martha for a considerable period of time with no word on her plans to return. It is entirely possible that Mary frequently leaves the premises to pursue her own ministry and Jesus knows her location.

Martha's question does not become so rhetorical if she is asking Jesus if he does not care that she is left alone to manage affairs by herself, while her sister is away somewhere. Jesus reassures her that Mary's choice is "good," and then chapter 11 starts with prayer. The summary of immediate topics, both preceding and following the Luke 10:38–42 pericope, hints at the reason that Mary had "left Martha alone." Mary could be one of the women following Jesus with other disciples or with "the seventy." Martha's response is to be reassured that Mary's choice is good.

It makes Martha seem less petty than if she is just prevailing upon Jesus to help her get Mary back into the kitchen, which is a rather small matter which the sisters could presumably settle on their own. Jesus says, to whomever is present, and to all of Luke's readers in the generations since, that Mary has made a good choice. This is not to imply that Martha is not doing good, and Jesus also does not say that Martha should be doing the same as Mary. Jesus approves and supports Mary's decision for her; he is not necessarily defending her against Martha's mode of service.

The new information gained in this chapter on Luke 10:38–42 will be carried into the following chapters of this book. If it appears that I am repeating myself, it is because this is a shock to our old conception of the story: Mary is away, gone from Martha. She does not speak, and is spoken of in the third person. Martha wants her back to help with her unspecified substantial responsibilities. Jesus knows where Mary is, because apparently it is in his power to convince her to return home.

If this narrative is taking place in Galilee, early in in Jesus' mission, then this is the time that Jesus is chosing his twelve disciples as well as other followers. Mary and Martha could have been among the earliest believers in Jesus. Therefore, they had time to develop a close friendship and Mary would have had time to develop a reputation herself as a repected teacher and leader of new converts out in the countryside with Jesus.

Considering the close proximity of a previous passage, Luke 9:57–62, in which Jesus describes the personal cost to be a disciple, leave family and to follow him, it is possible 10:38–42 is an illustration of this cost from the point of view of the family members left behind. At the beginning of Luke 10, Jesus sent out "the seventy." Mary could have been included in that number; at least there were many other families faced with loved ones leaving to spread the message. Suddenly, the old familiar Martha and Mary story has a whole new look, and doesn't seem like a silly spat between sisters.

Many new applications result from this new perspective on Luke 10:38–42. Mary and Martha are both known to be "sitters at the feet of Jesus, listening to his words." No longer is one sister setting an example to be emulated and the other stands to be corrected. With the multitudes of people following Jesus in his early ministry, there were many families faced with the absence of loved ones leaving home to evangelize.

What has changed in the application of this passage as a result of these findings? The sisters are not pitted against each other in such a way that one has correct priorities and the other is misdirected. A choice does not have to be made between contemplative and active discipleship. Yes, study at the feet of Jesus is still a priority. Both woman have permission to study and with evidence they indeed both have a history of being discipled with Jesus. On this particular day, as Luke records, reflection and quiet time is simply not the topic of discussion. That has been done, and will continue another day, but now the lesson is the practical application with hands and feet, which was learned at the feet of Jesus. We will see what that lesson becomes. No longer does Jesus appear to be contradicting himself by advocating selfless service in earlier passages, but then in the presence of Martha undermining her service. Martha's exact *diakonia* is unspecified and could be a variety of activities, but not limited to setting the table.

What hasn't changed is that the story is still about Martha and she still is the one that comes to a new realization. Now the learning is at a much deeper level; Martha is no longer fretting over serving duties, but is worried about the absence of her sister. Who cannot empathize with this dilemma? Jesus is still mediating a message between the sisters, but the message, the urgency, and the distance the message is conveyed has greatly increased. Instead of a message, "Don't you care that my sister has left me alone in the kitchen?" Martha asks Jesus, "Don't you care that my sister has left me alone to cope with many responsibilities at home without help, while she goes off to an unknown location in your service?" Martha shows much more depth of character if her great weakness is wanting her family member nearby, instead of getting over-involved with hostess duties.

Luke 8:19–21 is about forming a new family, "My mother and brothers are those who hear God's word and put it into practice." It is a lesson of discipleship and the many forms it takes and following at whatever the cost (Luke 18:29). Sometimes disciples minister within their familiar surroundings and this is a valid and demanding call, not all are called to leave, but others are called to serve in new locations.

A familiar theme is repeated, frequently taught by Jesus, that worry is never helpful and prayer is, whether or not the connection to the next chapter is intended or not. David Grummet brought up a challenging point: "To what extent have choices between variant readings of texts, including different manuscript sources, been determined by the theological agendas of expositors?"[44] I also suspect that a theological agenda has been conscienciously carried out: preconceptions of women's work and natures have certainly shaped the lessons that have been taught from Luke 10:38–42 to the discouragement of women. Mary and Martha have new lessons to teach and it is no longer about getting priorities right and the danger of getting caught up in superfluous housework. Suddenly, the old familiar Martha and Mary story has a whole new look, and several new lessons are brought forward for both men and women. As amazing as these findings are, the sisters have more to teach as we move into John and study the "anointing woman" pericopes.

---

44. Grummet, "Action and/or Contemplation?" 126.

PART II

4

The Johannine Mary and Martha

As introduction to the Johannine Mary and Martha, a few words are necessary to determine whether the four verses of Luke inform the much longer passage in John. Of particular interest in understanding Mary and Martha is the relationship between the two passages, Luke 10:38–42 and John 11:1—12:11. Is it legitimate to connect the two, or are the books two separate documents, written and read in separate historical audiences? A decision must be made on whether the two episodes, written by two different authors, are complementary, or must be read independently.

In the view of most scholars, at the time the Fourth Gospel was written, Matthew, Mark, and Luke were already in circulation and being read as true witnesses to the life and teachings of Jesus. How does one account for the material he omitted, that is known from the other Gospels, and what is the origin of the passages that are unique? Either the writer of John purposely chose not to include the information already written in the earlier Gospels because he assumed his intended readers already knew it, or he did not have access to the other Gospels in written or oral form.

DO LUKE AND JOHN KNOW EACH OTHER?

The writing of Luke-Acts may have been completed as early as A.D. 62,[1] or as late as the 70s or early 80s.[2] Luke most certainly precedes the writing of

1. Blomberg, *Jesus*, 171.
2. Witherington III, *The Acts of the Apostles*, 62.

John (A.D. 81–96).[3] That the author of John could realistically have had access to the Synoptics and his possible use of the texts of Matthew, Mark, and Luke is a complex discussion.[4] Much of the material of John is not known from any other source, yet the text co-exists well with the Gospels, and John often appears to fill in gaps in the knowledge.[5]

Prior knowledge is also presumed of the implied readers. Characters such as Andrew and Simon Peter (John 1:40) are not actually introduced but suddenly appear. Readers are assumed to know that in 3:24, John the Baptist will be imprisoned and they are familiar with the outcome of the story. One issue of particular concern in this study is the introduction of Mary with a typical "Johannine aside" in 11:2, "the one who anointed Jesus." She appears to be a familiar figure to the implied readers. It is very unlikely the author of John would use new characters without introduction if he did not think his intended audience already knew them.

One could consider that both Luke and the writer of John wrote independently of each other. Perhaps both Gospel writers personally knew the women and drew similar independent conclusions about their personalities. The opinions from commentaries range from no evidence that John was writing with knowledge of the other Gospels, to proposing that he was acquainted with the other documents and used them as sources. O'Grady confidently asserts: "Most scholars agree that there is no literary dependence on the other three. Any similarities can be attributed to a common oral tradition."[6] In contrast, Blomberg states: "The interlocking of stories between John and the Synoptics seems to indicate that John knew the other Gospels, but intended to elaborate rather than to repeat familiar material."[7] Dodd considers that although John is writing later than Luke, he is writing from his memory as a direct witness, so he is the most accurate.[8] As this monograph is written, I will agree with Dodd, Blomberg, and Davies who also adds, "Once we recognize that the Fourth Gospel retells a story already familiar to readers, the gaps are not so puzzling. The story is retold to

---

3. Blomberg, *Jesus*, 194.

4. For further discussion on the relationship of John to the Synoptics see Köstenberger, *John*, 17–18; Beasley-Murray, *John*, xxxv–xxxvii.

5. Blomberg, *The Historical Reliability*, 47–49.

6. O'Grady, *According to John*, 137.

7. Blomberg, *Jesus*, 179.

8. Dodd, *Historical Tradition*, 423–432.

emphasize the theological significance of Jesus' life, rather than to provide a full biography."[9]

The relationship between Luke's passage (10:38–42) concerning Mary and Martha, and the personalities of the women as described in John 11–12, may be an illustration of this cooperation between the authors. The pericopes appear to mesh well, with John adding information to that already known about the characters as portrayed in Luke. It is interesting to speculate if either Luke and/or the writer of John personally knew the sisters.[10] In both, Martha is articulate and upfront in conversation, while Mary remains mysterious and expresses herself not through discourse, but through actions. In Luke and John, Jesus praises Mary's behavior. Both sisters are willing to engage in the role of servant, even though their economic status did not require it. Mary washed Jesus' feet as if she were a servant and Martha is willing to serve as a hostess in John 12. Luke and John both portray them as devoted disciples and loved by Jesus.

The fourth evangelist certainly has taken the message and life of Christ, and written his own unique version apart from the other three. The relationship between the Gospels will remain an open discussion. I find the evidence that the writer of John was familiar with the prior canonical Gospels convincing. He also wrote as though his implied readers knew those characters well enough to elaborate on that information for a more complete portrait. Therefore, material from Luke 10:38–42 will be used in conjunction with John 11:1—12:11.

Having decided that Luke 10 can legitimately inform John 11–12, and given the findings of chapter 3, Mary and Martha take on a new complexion as we move forward. If one reads John with the preconception that Mary was the one who in the past "got it right," and Martha is the one who "fussed too much," then these results are inevitably carried over into the sisters' appearance in John 11 and the reader is going to look for traces of the same personalities in the new setting. With the new perspective of the sisters as we discovered in Luke, do the sisters have a fresh appearance as we resume their story in the Johannine pericope?

Moving over the bridge into the Gospel of John, one immediately notes different issues in exegesis compared to the Lukan passage. The reader has much more text to examine, compared to the four verses of Luke, but textual variants affect the reading very little, and grammar is

---

9. M. Davies, *Rhetoric*, 30.

10. Witherington III, *Women*, 112.

more straightforward. Because of the greater amount of text, literary devices are numerous, and reading from a narrative perspective becomes very informative. In the Johannine passage, careful study of selected vocabulary yields important insights. Again, I am sorting out the Greek study from the rest of the exegesis. Results will be integrated into the following section.

OBSERVATIONS FROM THE GREEK OF JOHN 11:1—12:11

A few grammatical and vocabulary insights come forward, but considering the length of the passage, the grammar discussion is not nearly as dense as in the much-shorter Lukan text. At John 11:1, Lazarus is introduced as being ἀπὸ "from" Bethany, ἐκ "from" the village of Mary and her sister Martha. Very few commentators have noticed the two different prepositions that are both translated "from," nor have they attached any significance to this grammatical feature. This is not noticeable in the English translations and any importance is minimized by at least one commentator.[11] I propose that it could be further validation of the thesis pursued in the Lukan story that Mary and Martha were at home at an unnamed village, and not near Jerusalem. Lazarus was originally from the same village as his sisters, but Bethany is a more recent address.

The choice of ἠκολούθησαν "they followed" in verse 11:31 may suggest more meaning than just following Mary out of the house because they thought she was going to the tomb. The verb ἀκολουθέω is often used in the Gospels by Jesus when he says, "Follow me," in Luke 5:27 to Levi, in John 1:43 to Phillip, and in John 21:22 to Peter, which is a small sample.[12] According to Colleen Conway, the use of ἀκολουθέω may be an indication of Mary's role as a leader of the Jews, who, in following her out of the house, eventually come to belief in Jesus when they observe the miracle.[13]

Starting in John 11:33, three different verses describe Jesus' emotions. First, Jesus sees Mary and the Jews "crying." The evangelist describes Mary's sorrow with the verb κλαίουσαν, "crying" and the crowd of Jews with the same verb κλαίντος. This is the loud wailing and crying common to women in public displays of grief in that culture, and is a frequently used word for "crying" in the NT. "When Jesus saw her weeping," (11:33) provokes a vivid reaction from Jesus that creates translation challenges. He is said to

11. Köstenberger, *John*, 325 citing Brownlee 1972.

12. Kohlenberger III, *Concordance*, 25–26.

13. Conway, *Men and Women in the Fourth Gospel*, 145.

ἐνεβριμήσατο τῷ πνεύματι καὶ ἐτάραξεν ἑαυτόν. This is variously translated as by the NRSV "greatly disturbed and deeply moved," or in the TNIV, "he was deeply moved in spirit and troubled." The verb ἐμβριμάομαι in classical Greek describes the "snort of a horse in war or in a race."[14] For humans, it describes feeling strongly about something, or to be deeply moved.[15] Until this point in John, Jesus is not portrayed as expressing emotion, but in this scene he is seen as very human.[16] The use of such an unusual word to describe Jesus' crying is puzzling, and the meaning of Jesus' tears is very diversely interpreted.[17] Some commentaries see Jesus as troubled at his own impending death.[18] Because the word indicates strong emotions, Jesus is thought to bristle at his imminent encounter with and assault on death.[19] Others say he is sharing in Mary's grief.[20] The object of Jesus' strong emotions is not mentioned.[21] No indication is given that he is angry with either Mary or Martha for any reason such as excessive sorrow or lack of faith.

Elsewhere ἐμβριμάομαι has three uses in the NT meaning to "rage against" (Matt. 9:30, Mk. 1:43, Mk 14:5), showing an unexpressed but strong sense of vexation, or perhaps "be angry at."[22] The other uses of the word do not seem to have any similar use, being references from Matthew and Mark which are occasions when Jesus "strongly warns" the recipients of a healing miracle not to tell anyone. In Mark 14:5, surprisingly, the verb ἐμβριμάομαι is connected with the anointing woman, i.e., Mary, and describes the indignation of onlookers to the waste of precious ointment that could have been sold to help the poor. This parallel use of vocabulary between Mark and John 11 in connection with Mary gives me pause. As the onlookers to the anointing in Mark were indignant at the perceived waste of resources, Jesus is indignant at the sight of the mourning crowd.

---

14. Luther's translation is vivid, "*Ergrimmte er im Geist und ward betrübt in sich selbst.*" *Grimmen* is a cramp-like pain in the stomach, in this case, in his Spirit. *Trüben* is to be troubled or darkened.

15. BDAG, 322.

16. Yamaguchi, *Mary & Martha*, 117.

17. A good summary of opinions on why Jesus cried is found in Köstenberger, *John*, 340, n 92.

18. Culpepper, *Anatomy of the Fourth Gospel*, 111.

19. Köstenberger, *John*, 339.

20. Schneiders, "Death in a Community," 54.

21. Köstenberger, *John*, 340.

22. Kohlenberger III, *Concordance*, 251.

The active ἐτάραξεν ἑαυτόν is from ταράσσω[23] a common word meaning to "shake or stir up," or "to cause inward turmoil," and could be translated "he was troubled or agitated."[24] The evangelist has described Jesus in extraordinary stress. I would translate 11:33: "his spirit heaved and he trembled with rage." To determine exactly the quality and cause of Jesus' emotional state in this scene is a juggernaut that remains unsolved.

A few verses later another note of Jesus' emotional state occurs. The translation of 11:35, "Jesus wept," (ἐδάκρυσεν ὁ Ἰησοῦς), a verb used only here in the NT,[25] is too mild and leaves the impression that Jesus was merely weeping. The Greek word δακρύω is unusual with only extra-biblical uses noted.[26] I like the comment from O'Day and Hylen who note, "It is important not to sentimentalize Jesus' reaction and his tears. Jesus responds to the power of death he sees around him."[27]

The action at 11:43 has moved to the tomb, where "he shouted" (ἐκραύγασεν) with a "loud voice" (ψωνῇ μεγάλη): "Lazarus, come out!" The verb used here, κραύγαζω is different from the verb for "to cry out" in 7:37 (κράζω). Whereas κράζω is appropriate for "inspired proclamation," the strong verb κραύγαζω is used nine times in the NT,[28] always referring to "loud shouting" of a person or crowd. The word will occur in key scenes: e.g., John 12:13 as Jesus enters Jerusalem where the crowds wave palms shouting, "Hosanna!"; "Give us Barabbas" (18:40); "Crucify!" (19:6); "Take him away! Crucify Him!" (19:15). The use of this verb raises the intensity and emotional sounds of Jesus' trial. The same verb choice in John 11:43 describes an earth-shaking roar that robs the tomb of death.

Textual issues in John 12:1–11 are not numerous and do not impact possibilities for interpretation as much as in Luke 10:38–42. The only variant of some interest concerns the exact description of the λίτραν μύρου νάρδου πιστικῆς "pound of myrrh nard, precious," that Mary used to anoint the feet of Jesus and its monetary value.[29] Jesus' exact phrase to Judas, "Let

23. Kohlenberger III, 990.

24. Kohlenberger III, 805.

25. Kohlenberger III, 139.

26. BDAG, 211.

27. O'Day and Hylen, *John*, 117.

28. Kohlenberger III, *Concordance*, 439.

29. See Esler and Piper, *Lazarus, Mary and Martha*, Appendix 2 pp 165–177. They have researched the variants and come up with a translation, "When Mary had taken a pound of best quality, a precious lotion, she anointed the feet of Jesus."

her be," is also subject to diverse translations. While the phrases are interesting in their own right, they will not be pursued here.

To summarize, this exegesis of selected key vocabulary from John 11:1—12:11 is not as decisive as that from Luke. An important item is Mary's importance in leading the Jews out of the house to Jesus, indicated by the same verb that Jesus used when he was calling the disciples. The variety of verbs used to express the range of grieving raises the emotional impact of the passage. Unique vocabulary indicates that Jesus was very emotionally involved in this scene with Mary and the Jews who followed her out of the house. Considering the choice of words, the sound of his voice must have made a profound memory on the observers who retold it. The cause of this outburst and the reason that Jesus cries remains a mystery, although there are many possibilities. The text gives no hints, only the observation of the Jews who say, "See how he loved him." It is unknown whether this is an accurate observation of the source of Jesus' emotions or an illustration of how misguided the Jews were. One thing is certain, that Jesus was humanly affected by the tragedy of the scene and his reaction was precipitated by Mary's falling at his feet and crying loudly.

The results of the vocabulary study illustrate how the author increased the sense of drama by choosing unique descriptive words, particularly for the aural impression of the scene. Especially notable is Jesus' involvement as a human, who loved as a human, and felt sorrow at the death of his friend that he loved. He was not a disinterested participant estranged from the action. Mary and Martha, as well as the crowd, observed his human emotions, which seem to be precipitated initially by Mary's crying.

CONTEXT IS IMPORTANT

Within the larger context of the Fourth Gospel, the Lazarus story is climatic because it is the culminating sign of Jesus that leads directly to his condemnation by the Jewish rulers and his eventual arrest and sentence. Many commentators note the central importance of this pericope to the whole Gospel. It forms both a conclusion to Jesus' public ministry and a preparation for John's passion narrative. Culpepper calls 13:1 "the most significant transition in the Gospel."[30] He sees this as achieved literarily by the conjunction of the two systems of time present throughout the narrative, the pattern of Jewish feasts, and the approach of Jesus' hour. "The

30. Culpepper, "The Johannine *Hypodeigme*: A Reading of John 13," 133–149.

raising of Lazarus is a great hinge in the plot of the Gospel."[31] Lazarus' raising from the dead sets in motion the plot to put Jesus to death. Caiaphas
inadvertently says it best, "You know nothing at all! You do not realize that
it is better for you that one person die for the people than that the whole
nation perish" (11:50–51). The plot advances towards its denouement with
renewed vigor, "from that day on they planned to put him to death." The
narrative itself, 11:1—12:11 can be seen as a unit in a chiastic structure with
the raising of Lazarus as the center.[32] The Lazarus story, as the longest sign
account, is skillfully woven into the larger Gospel.

The Lazarus pericope develops several themes that were anticipated in
previous chapters.[33] These include qualities of discipleship, impending danger to Jesus heightened by the threats of the Jews, and Jesus as the bringer
of life. A friend lays down his life for a friend, is another theme, as Jesus
knowingly raised Lazarus, with the realization he would be closer to death
himself. The all-embracing theme is belief in Jesus, as we see it in 10:42;
11:42; and 20:30–31.

Mary and Martha continue a pattern of discipleship as noted earlier. John 11:1—12:11 is preceded by Jesus' discourse on discipleship in
10:22–42 where he healed a blind man. The Pharisees called the formerly
blind man to the temple and questioned him harshly. They claimed to be
disciples of Moses, but do not know Jesus, who worked the miracle, because
they do not know whose disciple he is. The now-sighted man says that this
miracle worker can only be from God, "If this man were not from God,
he could do nothing" (9:33). This healed man becomes spiritually more
progressively enlightened as his eyesight returns, as also do the recipients
of other discourses, e.g., Nicodemus, (3:1–15), and the Samaritan woman
(4:1–26). Martha, as shown by her words, and Mary as shown by her actions, also become progressively more enlightened. These texts preceding
chapters 11–12 anticipate the themes of the Johannine passages concerning
Mary and Martha.

As we review the context of 11:1—12:11, the following chapters
continue to develop the themes introduced. Beirne draws a narrative observation by noting that although Mary does not personally reappear in
the narrative after 12:8, she throws a shadow across the following chapters. As she anointed Jesus' feet, so also in 13:1–30 Jesus washes the feet

31. Ressiguie, *Strange*, 186.

32. Lee, *Flesh and Glory*, 199.

33. Köstenberger, *John*, 357–358.

of the disciples. As she prepared him for burial and applied ointment, so also in 19:39–40 is the anointing by Nicodemus.[34] These later scenes further amplify Mary's act of anointing. Mary's role as a model of discipleship is extended and affirmed. The literary links between the two anointing stories in John (cf. Mary's and Nicodemus's) also suggest that the second literally completes the first; they are two stages in the embalming process.[35] In both scenes, a disciple of Jesus braves the comments of bystanders by initiating the loving task of preparing Jesus' body for burial, the first in anticipation, the second in reality.

34. Beirne, *Women and Men*, 160.

35. Beirne, *Women and Men*, 154.

5

Life Was Different in the First Century

CHAPTER 4 BEGAN THE transition into the book of John by noting the relationship between the two Gospels, and the legitimacy of using one to inform the other. The most interesting Greek vocabulary was studied, and the location of the Mary, Martha, Lazarus pericopes set into their context with the rest of the Gospel of John. In chapter 5 I am again picking up social-cultural items of particular interest to the Johannine passage.

HONOR WAS SERIOUS BUSINESS

Women were making some gains in freedom of movement, divorce, and economic gains during the first century, but the honor-shame standards were still alive and well. Behavior standards were very much maintained; a demeanor of shame was appropriate for women but not required for men. Women were required to show modesty, restraint, discretion, and above all, purity.[1] An accusation of "shamelessness" would bring social ruin to a woman. Deference was shown to men, but economic status trumped gender, and aristocratic women could get away with much more, not being required to defer to lower-ranked men. As we look at the Gospel stories of the anointing women these societal requirements will be important considerations.

Men were also heavily invested in the honor-shame culture, but Jesus set the example of how these customs would be dismantled. Men were expected to maintain public honor and not be humiliated—especially by

1. Arlandson, *Women, Class, and Society*, 156.

someone of lower rank. To be "bested" by a woman would be to risk loss of credibility among his peers as well as those over whom he had power. Jesus discredits many powerful men in the course of his ministry by means of raising the status of a woman at a man's social expense.

Normally a brother would be expected to help his sister, but in the case of John 11, the sisters are free agents with no male head of household. At the very beginning of the Lazarus pericope, this tendency is already apparent in 11:1 as taking place "in the village of Mary and her sister Martha." Worth noting is that the male character is introduced by his relationship to the female characters, contrary to typical Greco-Roman literature.[2] In that culture it was unusual that the sisters were taking the initiative in the care of the male member of the family, contrary to the customs in patriarchal family structures.

Further, they seek help for their dying brother by appealing to Jesus, an unrelated man. When Jesus arrives in Bethany, Mary could be viewed as exhibiting more appropriate female decorum by remaining in the house until Jesus called for her. Martha broke the rules when she went out to Jesus unbidden. Moving ahead to chapter 12, the honor code was broken during the Johannine dinner, where apparently women and men ate together, Martha hosted, Mary anointed and loosened her hair, all breaches of gender and societal roles. The social code is maintained between Jesus and the disciples until he defends Mary against a male disciple, Judas. In John 13, the code is again undermined when Jesus follows a female disciple's example of behavior by washing his disciples' feet, who would be his social subordinates.[3]

DINING IN PRONE POSITION

Unlike Luke 10 where I conclude that dining is not part of the picture, John 12:1–8 certainly is a dining scene. The banquet illustrated pre-Christian ideology such as: creating community, defining behavior, sharing values, and connecting with the divine.[4] At this time in the Mediterranean world, women and men reclined at formal meals, and data indicates that even for the Passover *seder* many elements from the Greco-Roman symposium had

2. Kim, *Woman and Nation*, 142.

3. Yamaguchi, *Mary & Martha*, 136.

4. Smith, *From Symposium* 279.

been incorporated.[5] Most households, even those of peasants, would have at least one maidservant.[6] If servants were available, then householders would be served at meals and therefore recline to eat, which would not be possible if they had to do the serving themselves. Some meals in which Jesus participated contain elements of the typical Greco-Roman traditions.

Dining customs gathered from the Gospels include some interesting details. All of the meal scenes in Mark describe male diners as reclining, e.g., Levi's house (Mk 2:15); outdoors (6:39; 8:6); and Simon's house (14:15, 18). Mark also mentions the reciting of prayers (Mk 6:41; 8:6–7), and drinking of wine (Mk 14:23). Luke offers more urbane details as in 7:36–50 when Jesus dines with Simon the Pharisee and asks why he was not given water to wash his feet, oil for his head, and a kiss of greeting. In Luke 14:7 Jesus tells a parable of sitting according to rank: "He noticed how guests picked out the places of honor at the table."[7] Many different variables as servants, guests, and the level of formality, complicate the accurate imaging of the setting of John 12:1–8. These descriptions from the other Gospels provide details in dining that would be familiar to Jesus' world.

There are still many unknowns concerning the dinner event with Martha as the hostess. Martha's function (ἡ Μάρθα διηκόνει), "Martha served," whether she served or was the hostess, or some combination of activities, is an item left to the imagination. John 2:2 starts with ἐποίησαν "they made." The reader is given no indication of who "they" are; no more hints as to the opulence and formality of the event are offered. In Jerusalem, villas have been uncovered that feature every luxury known to Greco-Roman culture.[8] Bethany was a short distance removed; yet, whether such homes existed that would support a banquet type dinner in Bethany is unknown. It appears that the economic status of the household in Bethany would sustain a formal δεῖπνον "dinner." Judging from the value of the perfume Mary used, the biblical sources do not hint of financial scarcity in the family.

Is it possible that the sisters would not be at the table during a dinner celebration in honor of their dear friend, Jesus, but only standing in the background? One would think that such an important family event would include mention of Martha and Mary as honored guests at the table. It may seem that the only way they had access to the festivities was by serving, or

---

5. Jeffrey, *Luke*, 111.

6. Corley, *Private Women*, 15.

7. Smith, *From Symposium*, 222.

8. Meyers, "The Problems of Gendered Space," 51–58.

illicitly "breaking and entering" as Mary did when she apparently without prior planning or permission from anyone, anointed the feet of Jesus. Mary's presence would be tolerated only if she was sitting silently at the feet of Jesus as a dutiful wife would sit at the feet of her husband at a banquet.[9] Certainly at the Passover Seder, which was a family event, Jewish customs replaced the customs of the Greco-Roman "symposia," which more likely allowed men and women to dine together. Banquets were also held in someone's honor like a birthday or anniversary, and the event in Bethany would probably fall closer to that category.[10] As an aside, it would not be the last time that women were barred from the table.

This discussion of dining customs concludes that the event of John 12 was a formal affair at an unidentified house, because reclining at the table is mentioned (12:2). Most likely, Martha is the hostess in the sense she planned the event and she directed the servants who are doing the actual labor. If the spaciousness of the house allowed for a "reclining dinner" then the economic status of the householder would probably support several servants. This was a company of close friends including men and women reclining, if not together at the same table, then at different tables in the same room. Whether Mary had preplanned the anointing, and had a container hidden in her skirts, or if her action was spontaneous, is unknown. Whatever Mary's position at the table, reclining with the men, sitting at Jesus' feet, or if she crept in later unbidden, remains speculative.

ANOINTING ETIQUETTE

Because the anointing concludes with Mary wiping Jesus' feet with her hair, conclusions concerning the customs of footwashing and hairstyles will be considered together. When does simple foot care acquire the designation of an "anointing?" What is the significance if hair is used as a wiping material instead of a towel?

It is understandable that the washing and care of feet was important in the hot, dusty world of first-century Palestine. Feet were washed as part of rituals, for purposes of hygiene, hospitality, most typically being the service of a slave before a meal or other occasions.[11] Most guests took care of their own feet after a walk and the host would provide the necessary basin, water,

9. Corley, *Private Women*, 135–136.

10. Cohick, *Women*, 87.

11. Yamaguchi, *Mary & Martha*, 123.

and oil. A slave would perhaps be available to wash feet of guests. Mary would not normally assume the role of a servant and care for a guest's feet, but the practice "is not unknown in a Jewish household where in cases of deep love or extreme devotion a host or loved one might wash the feet of another."[12] The fact that Mary cared for Jesus' feet displays her utter devotion to him.[13] Therefore the washing of feet could pass from a purely functional necessity of hygiene, to a courtesy extended to a guest, to an intimate expression of devotion to someone beloved using luxury products.

In antiquity, the setting for washing feet was before the meal at the dining couch. The guests were in a reclining position on couches around a low table and left their sandals outside. The servant washing the guests' feet would not be bowed down in front of the guest or under a table. As everyone positioned their bodies at right angles to the table, the servant would go around the perimeter of the room and sit on the floor at the end of a couch to wash each guest's feet.[14] For a ready-made example of how footwashing would typically be master-servant duty, we need only to look to John 13:6–9 at Peter's reaction. When Jesus started washing Peter's feet, Peter objected, for that was too lowly a service to receive from his Lord. In the words of John the Baptist (Mark 1:7), he was not worthy to loosen the straps of Jesus' sandals. According to Midrash, washing feet was the job of a slave, but not required of a Jewish slave. Attending to another's feet was very lowly service.

Footwashing was typically followed by rubbing the feet with olive oil or a fragrant ointment, the verb referring to the action is ἀλείφω "anoint, pour, put oil on."[15] As soon as the action moved beyond a purely perfunctory action of cleanliness performed by a servant, it took on greater meaning. Jerome Neyrey presents an excursus on footwashing, which distinguishes between rituals and ceremonies.[16] Mary, in John 12 is confirming her love of Jesus in a ceremony of anointing his feet. When Jesus washes the feet of the disciples in John 13, he is performing a ritual, which changes their status into public witnesses of Jesus' passion and message. The disciples in

---

12. Beirne, *Women and Men in the Fourth Gospel*, 38.

13. Koester, *Symbolism in the Fourth Gospel*, 128.

14. Lee, *Flesh and Glory*, 267, n6.

15. Kohlenberger, *Concordance*, 214.

16. Neyrey, *The Gospel*, 356–376. Footwashing as a ritual indicates a one-time change of status such as baptism, marriage, ordination, or death. Ceremonies confirm roles and statuses such as anniversaries, temple rites, annual games, and feast days.

turn are to practice washing the feet of each other as a ceremony to confirm their standing.[17]

How does the scene change when a woman who is not a servant, unexpectedly uses her hair to dry the feet of a guest as occurs in John 12? One social-cultural item that has remained constant over the millennia is fascination with women's hair, by both men and women, although it is no longer as deadly seductive as it apparently was in the first century. A wide assortment of claims are made by various sources concerning the requirements of hair styles for first-century Jewish women. Most agree that Jewish women were required to keep their heads covered, although Keener states that the custom would apply only for married women.[18] I Corinthians 7:11 is cited to claim that the sight of loosened hair is for a woman's husband only. Rabbinical evidence claims that for a woman to loosen her hair in male company was to send clear sexual signals and so be judged as behaving disgracefully.[19] A woman's hair is her "glory" only to be enjoyed by her husband. According to Levitical law in Numbers 5:11–30, a woman accused of unfaithfulness is to be taken to the priest who would uncover her hair.[20]

An example of a woman loosening her hair and feet-kissing in first century pagan worship is illustrated in a Greek novel *Chaereas and Callirhoe* where upon return of her husband, the heroine puts her hands and face on the feet of the statue in the temple of Aphrodite. She lets down her hair and kisses the stone feet while crying, "Thank you, Aphrodite!"[21] Another non-canonical example is from the love story of *Joseph and Aseneth*, which describes her washing her husband's feet out of great devotion and love. In a first-century work by Petronius, *Satyticon*, a diner wipes excess oil from his hands onto the hair of servants.[22] The actions of Mary could possibly be understood in the context of novels of that genre, at least by the historic readers at the time John was written.

The conclusion from this research on women's hair and footwashing activities is that if washing the feet of an honored guest had precedents,

---

17. Neyrey, *The Gospel*, 358.

18. Keener, *John*, 863.

19. Beirne, *Women and Men*, 154.

20. Keener, *Paul, Women & Wives*, 39.

21. Vinson, *Luke*, 237.

22. Petronius, *Satyricon*, 27. For an enlightening, but not essential introduction to the debauchery of Roman dining, probably during the time of Nero, look up a synopsis of the plot.

then Mary's act of washing the feet of Jesus with precious ointments may have been understandable. The unexpected—and potentially scandalous—part of the scene in John 12 is that she loosened her hair to wipe his feet after anointing them with the precious perfume.[23] Koester notes that: "Most readers would have been able to understand Mary's actions as a display of devotion."[24] All of these actions taken together were sure to be remarkable to the other guests if not downright scandalous, even before the verbal exchange with Judas ensued.

DEATH IN BETHANY

Many important pieces of information apply to the Lazarus narrative. In Jewish practice, bodies were buried within twenty-four hours of death and the mourning procession took place following burial. Men and women walked separately in the procession as a ministry of love to the mourning family, an obligation that Jews valued highly and they laid much stress on the proper fulfillment.[25] Normally the anointing of the feet of the deceased would have been the task of the closest female relative.[26] After the burial, women returned from the grave to begin a thirty-day mourning period. The Talmud prescribes seven days of deep mourning, which would include loud wailing and dramatic displays of grief, and thirty days of light mourning. Even poor families were expected to hire two flute players and a wailing woman, which provides the aural backdrop for the burial scenes.[27] Relatives visited the grave of the newly deceased to assure that they were really dead. It was believed that the soul returned to the body every day for three days to determine if the body returned to life. After four days with no signs of life, the soul left for good.[28] This fact was added to the text to show there was no possibility of fraud, and the state of decomposition of the body was not an obstacle to the power of Jesus to perform this sign.

The verse (11:38) refers to Lazarus' tomb as a "cave" (σπήλαιον), which does not indicate a well-established wealthy family, who would have had a

---

23. Köstenberger, *John*, 361–362.
24. Koester, *Symbolism in the Fourth Gospel,* 127.
25. Ridderbos, *The Gospel According to John,* 393.
26. Yamaguchi, *Mary & Martha,* 137.
27. Köstenberger, *John,* 338.
28. Beasley-Murray, *John,* 189.

centuries-old above-ground tomb of interlocking chambers.[29] Perhaps the family was wealthy, but had not lived in Bethany for many generations to have built an impressive tomb.[30]

It was customary for those mourning the loss of a loved one to be sitting *shiva*.[31] The grieving household would receive condolences from visitors in a seated position.[32] Because friends and relatives would gather to console the family, a large group of mourners provided a large audience to witness the sign. The mention of a large number of Jews coming from Jerusalem indicates the prominence of the family, with additional mention that they came because of Mary (11:45). It is significant that Martha deliberately broke *shiva* to meet Jesus, but Mary was more reluctant to leave until Jesus called for her. Because Mary stayed in the house according to *shiva* which lasted seven days, she attracted attention when Jesus called for her. In addition to whatever prior knowledge these fellow Jewish mourners had of Jesus, those sitting with her would observe that Jesus was a very close and influential friend to her.

WHO ARE THE JEWS?

"The Jews" are mentioned prominently in John 11–12 and appear to influence every event. On the one hand, it is important to realize that all of the main characters of the Gospel are ethnic Jews. Brant points out that "throughout the Fourth Gospel, the Jews appeal to collective experience and traditions in their attempts to make sense of what they witness."[33] The disciples, the family at Bethany, and others who do not reject Jesus are also Jews. They frame their understanding of Jesus within Jewish tradition throughout John. Thus, we see that among the disciples, Andrew claims, "We have found the Messiah," (1:41) and Nathanael exclaims, "Rabbi, you are the Son of God! You are the King of Israel!" (1:49). Peter calls Jesus "the

29. Yamaguchi, *Mary & Martha*, 133.

30. In connection with the geographic findings above concerning the location of the Luke 10:38–42 pericope, perhaps the family's roots were northeast of Galilee, but they had recently moved to Bethany for the health of Lazarus. Bethany was the location of an Essene leper colony.

31. Keener, *The Gospel of John*, 842. The Jews mourned for seven days by sitting *shiva* at their house while receiving condolences from friends and relatives.

32. Köstenberger, *John*, 334.

33. Brant, *Dialogue and Drama*, 186.

Holy One of God" (6:60). On the other hand, after Jesus and the disciples receive the news of Lazarus's illness, they express worry about Jesus' safety as they attempt to dissuade Jesus from returning to Jerusalem, "because the Jews recently tried to stone him" (11:8). Ominously, Thomas builds more tension by pointing out that the Jews likewise threaten the lives of the disciples. To complicate matters, Jews have come out from Jerusalem to comfort the grieving family, but some of them also report Jesus' actions back to the Pharisees (11:46).

Throughout the Gospel of John, the first-century Jews are a varied group, and their role as support or enemy to Jesus' objectives is confusing. Different commentators make various distinctions. Davies sees geographic origin as the distinguishing characteristic, and the context must always be taken into consideration.[34] Sometimes the Jews refer to crowds who saw and heard Jesus, either in Galilee or in Judea. These Jews are like Jesus himself and are distinguished from the Samaritans. Other times Galileans are distinguished from Jews who are Judeans, Jesus' own people, although he is said to come from Nazareth (1:45).

Another interpretation of the Jews by Resseguie notes at least four ways that the term, "the Jews," is used in the Fourth Gospel: "neutral, hostile, positive, and symbolic."[35] The neutral usage includes festivals and rites where the term identifies special occasions. One of many examples is the "Passover of the Jews" in 2:13 or the "burial customs of the Jews," as identified in 19:40. Another neutral use includes "the Judean countryside" found in 3:22. Hostile Jews comprise the second use, which refers to the Jewish authorities. The phrase "for fear of the Jews" in 7:11–13 must be a reference to the Jewish authorities. John 9 illustrates both a neutral and hostile reference to the Jews.[36] In 9:13, 15, and 16, the Pharisees question the blind man, but in 9:18 the Jews did not believe him and in 9:22 the Jews excommunicated anyone who confesses Jesus. The third use of "the Jews" is positive as 8:31 describes Jews "who believed in Him." The fourth sense is symbolic, such as "the Jews" as representatives of the unbelieving world.

Critical for the development of my thesis is a distinction made by R. Brown. He distinguishes a category of Jews, which he calls "Crypto-Christians," who were believers, but they did not publicly profess Jesus out of

---

34. Davies, *Rhetoric and Reference*, 291.
35. Resseguie, *The Strange Gospel*, 127.
36. Resseguie, *The Strange Gospel*, 128.

fear.[37] They were non-confessing, and remained with the synagogue because a confession would have had them expelled. Another important group in John 11–12 is those Jews who were believers publicly, but lacked real faith or knowledge (John 6:66). Perhaps Jesus was explicitly trying to draw these "closet believers" into a public confession by his carefully planned and choreographed entry into Bethany. When he called Mary to him from the house crowded with Jews from Jerusalem, they were literally coming from the enclosed house out into the open. Or, perhaps Jesus was hoping that those with an incomplete knowledge would come out to him for further instruction, for example, as the man who was born blind in John 9 who publicly proclaimed his faith.

The frequent mention of "the Jews" throughout John 11 makes determining the status of the different categories of Jews an important issue. Some Jews are openly supportive and friends of Mary and Martha (11:19, 31, 33); others express skepticism and antagonism (11:36–37, 46); and in 11:45, 12:11 many Jews put their faith in him. Some are probably just curious or seeking sensation (12:9). It is important to determine how the author maximizes the potential contact between Jesus and the Jews who are reluctant to come out into the open and commit to him, and the roles Mary and Martha play to make this happen.

This brings to a conclusion some of the preliminary information necessary to understand this text in its cultural context. Special vocabulary that adds to better understanding of the scene, especially Jesus' emotional reactions, completes the picture. Just in case you are ever invited to a first-century event, be informed as to what to expect at a dinner party, or at a funeral, and be sure to keep your proper place in society in mind. It is a different world, and this is only scratching the surface; further study of first-century life in Judea pays off in many ways in better understanding.

37. Brown, *The Community of the Beloved Disciple*, 71.

6

Who Is Reading and Writing?

WITH VOCABULARY STUDY AND immersion into customs of the first century behind us, chapter 6 and chapter 7 go into the construction of the texts. Many details in the narratives themselves reveal much information about the original author and audience. Chapter 7 discusses many literary devices that are common especially to the Gospel of John and deepen the understanding of Mary and Martha. I have written a carefully abbreviated review of narrative concepts important to applying the texts that enlighten Mary and Martha.

AUTHOR AND READERS

Imagine you are an author with a writing utensil at your desk; this makes you the historical author. Unless you are writing an accurate autobiography, the character you create as an author may resemble you, or perhaps not. This character is totally your work, and you may legitimately deceive the reader about your real identity unless you are explicitly claiming to write truthfully about yourself. For instance, a man may ghost-write a biography of a woman, and may even claim, as a character or narrator, to be the main-character woman writing her own story as the truth.

In John 21:24, the narrator who calls himself the "beloved disciple," also claims to be the historic writer—or was this a fiction to increase the historic writer's credibility? Now, I am assuming something about you, the readers or intended audience of this book, that you believe in some level of inspiration of the Bible, and the human author of John was not out to deceive us. So, we take him at his word. How did the historic author, who claims to be the beloved disciple, with a true testimony, get his information? Was he an eye-witness or did he interview people who remembered? Who witnessed the interactions of Mary and Martha, or to whom did they talk? These are all the questions pursued in this chapter.

The Historic and Implied Author

My findings on the characters of Mary and Martha are primarily the result of narrative criticism, which reads the text as given, and does not seek to determine layers of editing or the historical author.[1] The historic writer creates a narrative, which omits less useful features of a story, and highlights the important elements to make his/her point. In the last verse of John (21:25), the author admits to this process: a "world full of books" that could have been written about the works of Jesus. This author had to determine how to streamline the vast amount of material. Narrative critics do distinguish between the historic author and the implied author who is revealed in the text, but this is difficult in the case of the Johannine author who only identifies himself as the "beloved disciple." The historic author is introduced here only so the clear contrast can be made with the implied author.

The implied author is the image of the author constructed in the mind of the reader from the narrative alone, without information from outside resources.[2] The terminology, "implied author," when speaking of the Gospel of John is an easy concept to understand. Because the historic author(s) is truly unknown, Johannine scholars have been habitually working with the concept of "implied author."[3] Outside of inconclusive historic tradition, information gathered from the text itself is the only information available about the historic author, and that is the definition of "implied author." Remember that "John" as the title of the Fourth Gospel was added later. In this work, the concept of "implied writer" is referred to as "the implied author," "the evangelist," and "the writer of John," as sort of catchall terminology.

---

1. For discussion on the historical writer of John see Blomberg, *Historical*, 22–41; see also Köstenberger, *John*, 7, n16.

2. Culpepper, *Anatomy*, 43–49.

3. Tovey, *Narrative Art*, 37.

The Historic and Implied Readers

The actual historic readers are, like the historic author, not of particular concern to the narrative critic. The possible identities of the ancient readers that actually picked up the hand-written documents are discussed in any commentary on Luke and John. Included with the historic readers are we, the readers of the twenty-first century. It is a challenge to think if the historic author could have imagined that he was writing for readers two thousand years hence! The modern reader must take on the world environment of the implied readers for an accurate reading, which is the reason for so much cultural and historical background study. Therefore, a twenty-first century, female reader of John must take on the worldview of the probable reader which was primarily a first-century, Greek reading, male audience. A wider audience would be reached when the work was read aloud to assemblies. To read authentically, modern readers must immerse themselves in first-century societal values, political realities, family structures, and language. We have briefly—too briefly— covered many of these topics in prior chapters. Deeper study in additional sources will richly increase understanding. The hazards of reading twenty-first values into the first century are great.

Narrative critics look for hints stated by the narrator in the text as to the identity of the audience imagined by the author during writing.[4] The implied reader is distinct from any historic reader in the same way that the implied author is distinct from the historic author. The historic author is making decisions about what his/her target audience already knows during writing. From the text of John, it can be determined that they were a believing community (20:31), which confessed its beliefs in God's purpose (1:14, 16–18).

The implied or intended reader of the Gospel of Luke is clearly identified, Theophilus, and purpose: "to draw up an account of the things that have been fulfilled" (Lk 1:1–4). The Gospel of John, in contrast, leaves us guessing. The intended reader(s) are not clearly stated in the text, so other hints must be scrutinized. The book could have been written for non-believers as a missionary tract, for a distinct group of believers, or for the church at large.[5] If written to Christians, then the original readers were possibly dispersed Jewish-Christians who moved to Ephesus, as the result of the Roman destruction of Jerusalem A.D. 70. Twenty or more years could have passed and the memory of Jerusalem has faded, so they need to be reminded of geographic

---

4. Powell, *What is Narrative Criticism?* 24.

5. Culpepper, *Anatomy*, 212.

locations. They may have had some knowledge of the LXX, probably had acquaintance with the Synoptics, and perhaps some of Paul's letters. Readers were expected to draw upon this knowledge and use it to supplement understanding as necessary when reading through the Fourth Gospel. They interacted with each other and their prior knowledge as they recognized familiar characters and added to their total understanding.

Although the author gives Jesus a long introduction in the prologue of the Gospel, he is known to the implied readers, although incompletely or inaccurately. Likewise, John the Baptist is known but not completely. The disciples are assumed to be known as "the twelve"; the "beloved disciple" is introduced as a known personality, but his special role as the author is new information.[6] Time and again, the Fourth Gospel gives the impression that it is retelling a story already somewhat familiar to its audience.[7]

Also distinguished are *narratees* who are named within the story.[8] Texts often indicate the nature of the audience anticipated by explicitly including the *narratees*, who are important to note in the particular pericopes studied here. The disciples are *narratees* when Jesus tells them about the nature of Lazarus' illness, walking in daytime and night, and their relationship to this man they call friend (11:4–14). Jesus' accompanying prayer (11:41–42) was for the benefit of those Jews who had come to console the sisters. Another example in John 12 would be the disciples at the dinner who are the witnesses of Mary's anointing and the recipients of the words of Jesus concerning his death. At the end of the Gospel, its readers are specifically admonished to play the same role as its *narratees* (20:31).

Very important to the pericope studied, Mary and Martha are somehow known to the implied readers, but a brother Lazarus is not. This is the first introduction of Lazarus as a unique character, formerly unknown to the readers of John or any Gospel. In John 11:2, the narrator intimates in an aside that some readers are already insiders, and have previous information concerning Mary. The discussion of how much the implied readers knew of the other Synoptics has been already undertaken, but one must consider the strong possibility that at least some readers are reading John before the other Gospels, therefore the characters are going to be unfamiliar to uninitiated historic readers, ancient and modern. Of particular interest to our inside look at Mary and Martha is the reason why the implied readers

6. Culpepper, *Anatomy*, 224.

7. M. Davies, *Rhetoric*, 357.

8. M. Davies., *Rhetoric* 359.

would be assumed to have prior knowledge of an anointing act by Mary, but are introduced to the miracle of the raising of Lazarus as though it is new information.

The Narrator

The narrator is important in this thesis because of the numerous "asides" he adds to the text, several of which are in the passages studied. The narrator observes Jesus and the disciples, and is free to interpret their minds. He is not limited to the position of the disciples and refers to them in the third person.[9] The narrator of the Fourth Gospel is omniscient, omnipresent, presumed reliable, and testifies to the reality depicted in the story (20:31 and 19:35, 21:24). He knows more about the characters than they may know about themselves. The narrator knows whom Jesus loves: "Now Jesus loved Martha, and her sister, and Lazarus." He points out "when the Jews . . . saw Mary rise . . . they followed her, supposing that she was going to the tomb" (11:31). In 11:33, "When Jesus saw her weeping, he was deeply moved in spirit and troubled," also, "Then Jesus, deeply moved again, came to the tomb" (11:38). The narrator also goes into the heads of the Jews, as in 11:45: "Many of the Jews . . . believed in him," and in 12:9, "When the great crowd of the Jews learned that he was there, they came, not only on account of Jesus but also to see Lazarus." The narrator knows the significance of a statement such as, "Jesus had spoken of Lazarus' death, but they thought that he meant taking rest in sleep" (11:13, also see 11:51–52, and 12:6). The narrator has complete control of the telling of the story. The narrator of the Fourth Gospel is an invisible, roving narrator.[10]

In summary, for the narrative critic, the complex discussion of the identity of the historic author and readers can be set aside. The implied author is only known from hints dropped in the text by the historic author. The text is the only source for knowledge of this usually fictional being, but in the case of this Gospel, the implied author turns out to be a real person and character of the narrative, the "Beloved Disciple." This disciple claims to narrate an accurate account of the words and actions of Jesus. The implied author is also the narrator who is part of a community of believers around Jesus. If the narrator and implied author are the same, and since

9. Culpepper, *Anatomy*, 27.

10. Culpepper, *Anatomy*, 139–140.

there is no reason to think the historic author is misrepresenting himself, then all three authors of the Gospel of John, could be interchangeable.

Point of View

How does the implied reader see the action? Resseguie defines point of view as "the way a story gets told."[11] The point of view, is the line of vision from which the content of the story is observed. The author's attitude or evaluation of characters is disclosed by the point of view. Several different points of view are possible, such as ideological, spatial, temporal, and psychological.[12]

Narrative criticism identifies how readers are expected to be affected by the text if it is read from the point of view that the text assumes the reader to possess.[13] The point of view of a narrator may be limited to what is in the head of one particular character in the story, or a narrator may be omniscient who observes all things crucial to the story. The nature of the Gospels is such that they are told from a third person, omniscient, all-seeing, point of view.

The psychological point of view is particularly well illustrated in the John 11:1—12:11 pericope. This point of view reinforces the narrative's ideological perspective.[14] As Jesus moves closer and closer to Lazarus's tomb, there is progressive heightening of the characters' emotions, which intensify as the tomb looms larger. When Jesus sees Mary and the Jews weeping, he is "greatly disturbed in spirit" and "deeply moved" at their response 11:33. The narrator notes that Jesus "began to weep" (11:35) and at the tomb he is again "greatly disturbed." The interior state of mind parallels other aspects of point of view. The narrative pace slows, and Jesus' voice rises to the loudest level ever. "All this allows the tomb, its emotional impact, and its dramatic reversal to take center stage. Everything builds to the one climactic moment when Lazarus comes out of the tomb."[15]

Since the vocabulary describing Jesus' voice is extensive, it draws attention to tone of voice as communicating a point of view. Jesus raises his voice at prominent points in the narrative to draw attention to new,

11. Resseguie, *Strange Gospel*, 1.

12. Resseguie, *Strange Gospel*, 4.

13. Powell, "Narrative Criticism," 246.

14. Resseguie, *Strange Gospel*, 17.

15. Resseguie, *Strange Gospel*, 17.

unfamiliar ideological perspectives.[16] His voice rises to majestic levels to call Lazarus back from the dead, and he "cries out" to summon all to come to him to satisfy their thirst. With each cry, an intensified point of view is underscored. This crescendo even continues to the climax of a heavenly voice-like thunder in 12:29.

The discussion in this section has sought to put the modern reader into a proper perspective concerning the ancient text. It is also important that the reader is familiar with the terminology about authors and readers, real or implied. Again, one must gauge the distance between the historic author and the historic events, whether the author was an eyewitness, or when and from whom he got the material. This may determine historical accuracy, but the author may have purposely redacted his material to make his argument stronger. How he presents the material and gets the point across through the narrator and point of view is in the artistry of the writing. Because these distinctions will occur frequently in the narrative analysis below of Luke 10:38–42 and John 11:1—12:11, these sections have been devoted to clarification.

PLOT AND STRUCTURE OF THE NARRATIVE

The author of John knows the tricks of the literary trade and uses them artfully. I have carefully narrowed down the selection of the following narrative devices that particularly target how the author emphasized certain aspects of the John 11–12 passages. These hints are easily overlooked, but if noted render important new information about our main characters.

Causal Links: Repetitions and Reversals

Causality describes the relationship between events and why one event is linked to another. This narrative is unique in that it is told in a reversed pattern from other miracle story examples in John and other Gospels. In the conversation that Jesus holds with Martha (11:21–27), the interpretation is given first in anticipation of the sign.[17] The author may have had Jesus give the explanation first to Martha, before the event is carried out, because he does not want any readers to miss the importance of the

16. Resseguie, *Strange Gospel*, 199.

17. Culpepper, *Anatomy*, 141.

sign.[18] The "signs" as revelations of Jesus are important to the movement and progress of the narrative.

Certain events are especially emphasized by repeated references in later passages. The Jews who mourn with Mary and Martha at Bethany mention the miracle of the man blind from birth (9:2–7). This reference (11:37) ties these Jews to those that witnessed the earlier dispute and the Jews who in 11:46 report Jesus to the authorities. After the raising of Lazarus, his name remains in memory by continued mention into the next chapter in verses 12:1, 9, and 17. Martha and Mary each greet Jesus with a repetition of the same remark, "If you had been here," which connects the two in either a contrasting or complementary way, which will be further discussed in the narrative analysis. If the reader looks carefully for hints, certain events are linked to indicate connection.

Conflict: The Drama Builds

Conflict refers to the way that the beginning and subsequent episodes anticipate its conclusion. The author of the Gospel of John is at his suspenseful best in John 11–12. An emotional connection is established at the opening verse with remembrance of a character already well known and loved, Mary. The author is telling the implied reader, "You should care about this person because this is someone you know." The main characters are in serious distress, someone is about to die, help is sought of Jesus; the reader is fully engaged and will not stop reading until the result is revealed.

The Lazarus story is one of the best examples of dramatic narrative timing. After the initial statement of the problem, that Lazarus is deathly ill, many verses are expended in explanation and discussion between Jesus and the disciples before leaving for Bethany, which builds up the suspense. Conflict is built up in the mind of the reader when Jesus says that the illness will not end in death, yet in a few verses Jesus states clearly that Lazarus is dead. The author emphasizes that Jesus loved the siblings, but then he remains in place for another two days without doing anything. Martha experiences conflict when Jesus does not come to Bethany within the expected time.

A conflict of some sort occurs at every turn of this story. The Jews follow Mary out of the house to see where she was going, because by leaving *shiva*, she indicated something extraordinary was happening. Martha is definitely conflicted about opening the grave because of the smell. The

18. Burge, *John*, 324.

reader recoils at the thought of the stench and reads faster to see what happens. Jesus' emotional outburst at Mary's appearance may be an indication of his conflict of emotions. In the next chapter, the witnesses of Mary's anointing were conflicted about her irregular appearance. Judas especially expresses his conflict by verbally objecting. At each of these points, the conflicts of the characters keep the readers riveted to the page.

Motifs: Crumbs Scattered in the Text

Motifs are used to structure the text by isolated, repeated words, and give indications of the Gospel's themes. It is worthwhile to notice the recurring vocabulary or leitmotifs. The "time" motif is probably the most frequently mentioned, starting with Jesus' reply to his mother, i.e., "My hour has not yet come" (2:4). In 7:6, Jesus discusses time as he travels to Jerusalem. Jesus certainly chose his own time to start the journey to the Lazarus event by waiting two days, with the result that Lazarus was in the tomb four days when he arrived in Bethany. In the text under consideration, a concentration of references to the feast of Passover occurs (e.g., 11:55 and 12:1). In 12:23, Jesus is aware that "the hour has come for the Son of Man to be glorified." The two major chronological markers running throughout the first part of John's Gospel (e.g., reference to Jewish festivals 2:13, 23; 4:45; 5:1; 6:4; 7:2; 10:22; 11:55; 12:1) and to Jesus' "time" (e.g., 2:4; 7:30; 8:20; 12:23,27; 16:32; 17:1), now merge in a Jewish festival that also marks the "time" of Jesus.[19] "Time" is a relentless, recurring motif throughout the entire Gospel that reminds the reader of impending crisis.

Calling someone by name is another motif that occurs frequently throughout the Gospel, as Martha calls Mary to come to Jesus outside the village at the request of Jesus (11:28), Jesus calls Lazarus out of the grave and out of death (11:43). Elsewhere in the Gospel, Jesus calls Mary Magdalene "Mary" (20:16). Like the sheep, Jesus knows his own and calls them by name. When he calls, they come (10:3).[20] Those who are closest to Jesus he calls by name. Recall in Luke how he called Martha by her name twice. The recipients of miracles in John are not generally named, but Lazarus is the exception. The brother and sisters were special people to Jesus whom he called his own.

19. Kitzberger, *Transcending*, 181.
20. O'Day and Hylen, *John*, 120.

An important theme is seen in the use of the verb, μένω "remaining or abiding," which occurs forty times throughout the Gospel.[21] Although the verb occurs only once in the passage and refers to Jesus "staying" where he was for another two days, this sets off the series of events causing his delay. Upon arrival, Martha greets him, "If you had been here." In other words, "If you had been with us, Lazarus would not have died."[22] As continued in his speeches of the next chapters, Jesus is teaching them that his physical presence is not necessary, but his spiritual presence is always with them.[23] The use of μένω is also serving to foreshadow the theme of chapter 15 when Jesus is speaking to the twelve. The message to them also applies to the sisters in their grief. Mary and Martha both play the illustrative roles of "abiding" as disciples in different ways. Mary is often seen to be the one who abides by the feet of Jesus (11:32, 12:3). Martha "abides" in his teaching and word (11:27). Both abide in positions as Jesus' students and disciples.

The motives of "time, calling, and abiding," are the most important examples of how John 11:1—12:11 are tied with the rest of the Gospel. Additional motives could be pointed out, but these examples indicate that Mary and Martha are performing integral parts of the message of faith and trust in the Gospel.

Timing of Events: When the Pulse Quickens

The author of John manipulates the pulse of the reader by varying the pace of the action. The way in which the length of the narrative is related to the time an incident would have occurred in the story provides its tempo. Events described in chapters 1–12 cover a period of two and a half years while chapters 13–19 focus on a mere twenty-four hours. Large gaps occur in the chronology of events, sometimes days pass without comment while other events are described in minute-to-minute updates. This is an example of great variation in tempo in John. The parts of the narrative that include speech most accurately approximate real time. Speech slows down the tempo of the narrative.

Examples where the dialogue slows down the pace occur at key points of the narrative as the Lazarus story is told. The dialogue carried on with the disciples before getting underway in travel to Bethany is a slow point,

21. Kohlenberger III, *Concordance*, 497.

22. Schneiders, "Death," 48.

23. Lee, *Flesh and Glory*, 88–109.

and the reader is anxious that action gets started (11:7–16). For the first sixteen verses, Jesus delays in going to Bethany for two days. In contrast, suddenly the travel time has gone by with no comment and Lazarus has been dead for four days. He is met by Martha and Mary outside of town who engage in conversations that require nearly double the verses, twenty-eight (11:17–44) and further decelerates the narrative pace, delaying Jesus' arrival at the tomb.[24] The last delay occurs at the tomb during Jesus' prayer of thanksgiving and Martha's short protest concerning the odor. By now, the reader is racing through the text to learn the outcome (11:40–41).

Martha receives greater priority in consideration of the actual time of action allotted to her because of the conversation with Jesus, in contrast to the apparent time allotted to Mary, which probably is less, depending on how long the "crying scene" requires. Martha again gets a short sentence at the gravesite. Considering the use of narrative time, Martha receives more priority in chapter 11. However, moving on to John 12, Martha receives only one phrase, "Martha served," (12:2), which could be considered background activity going on while Mary is featured. However, Mary is featured for the whole event, so considering both chapters together, Mary is ultimately the most memorable of the two sisters after chapter 12, so on basis of one measure, narrative time, Mary receives more emphasis.

Spaces and Settings: Where What Takes Place

Action in the Fourth Gospel is not confined to one place. Movement takes place between most events; the Fourth Gospel provides a travel itinerary and has many references to locations on a map. The passage of time is noted as progress is made through a landscape, which is the defining organizational principle of the Gospel.[25] Jesus is moving from the "other side of the Jordan" to close proximity to Jerusalem. The reader gets a sense of "coming home." "Crossing the Jordan" has a whole host of associations, as Joshua or Moses crossing the Red Sea, all of which could be applied here. In chapter 11 by itself, the operating space progressively narrows: in 11:1–16, Jesus is outside Judea; in 11:17–37, he is outside Bethany; and in 11:38–44, he is outside the tomb.[26] Jerusalem, with its associated threats, looms ever larger as the narrative progresses.

24. Resseguie, *Strange Gospel*, 9.
25. Brant, *Dialogue*, 41.
26. Stibbe, *John's Gospel*, 124.

Bookends are formed by 7:14 and 11:54. A progression has occurred between these two points. In chapter 7, Jesus declines to leave Galilee at the urging of his brothers, declaring that his time has not yet come, yet he leaves secretly. After arriving in Jerusalem on his own terms, Jesus spoke "openly" in the temple. At 11:54 he no longer "goes openly" among the Jews, but withdrew to Ephraim with his disciples. The turning point was when he met Martha and calls Mary out of the house into open space. He is notably still ministering in public until chapter 12.

Inside space is usually secure space, such as the "sheepfold" and "garden." Pilate wavering back and forth between inside and outside illustrates his indecision as compared to Jesus who remains steadfastly inside (18:28–40).[27] Similar to use of the "well" and "temple" earlier in the book, the tomb is the spatial and ideological center of John 11, finally reached after many obstacles such as unbelief and misunderstandings. Resseguie also points out that a psychological stance parallels the spatial stance and tension rises as the grave becomes closer.[28]

Unlike the "well scene" in chapter 4, in which Jesus remains stationary, in chapter 11 he travels through various degrees of resistance until he arrives at the tomb. Stibbe sees the travel to Lazarus' tomb as a "road of resistance" through unbelief and misunderstandings, which Jesus encounters before he confronts the greatest confinement, death.[29] As the spatial point of view progressively narrows to the tomb, the characters' responses become more passionate, the temporal pace slows down, and the misunderstandings to Jesus' point of view, occupy more and more narrative space.[30] The journey to his death is becoming ever more clear.

. Chapter 11 of John is all outdoors and the characters are mostly in motion and on their feet. The notable pauses include one for Martha, when she meets Jesus outside the village for the conversation, (11:20) and with Mary who falls at the feet of Jesus and weeps (11:32). With these exceptions, the entire chapter moves forward towards a larger event, which indeed occurs at the end of the chapter. The inside places, as inside the city of Jerusalem and inside the house where Mary is located with the Jews, are places of threat to Jesus because he does not know their intentions. The sign also occurs outside and Jesus brings Lazarus from inside the tomb to the

27. Resseguie, *Strange Gospel*, 86.

28. Resseguie, *Strange Gospel*, 90.

29. Stibbe, *John's Gospel*, 124.

30. Stibbe, *John's*, 124.

outside. In chapter 11, the interior is to be avoided. Chapter 12, in contrast, takes place in interior spaces where he is with those he loved and in a place a safety. Yet infiltration has occurred, Judas is also inside (12:4).

Whether a scene takes place in public space or private space is an important consideration that is also connected with the "shame/honor" code of the ancient Middle East as discussed above in chapter 5. A consideration of whether a scene takes place in public or private space concerns how gender roles are overstepped. Brant notices the use of female characters as they move from public to private, illustrating the divestment of power and authority in the public place and the increase of status to the private. This movement may be central to the presence of women and their characterization in this Gospel.[31]

Complicating matters is that Jesus blurs the division between the spaces, because he invites all his male and female disciples to be part of an "inner circle," or a sphere of fictive kinship.[32] In this inner circle of believers, males share food and beverage with females, as with the woman at the well. Jesus said to her "give me to drink" and they exchange information when she asks, "Are you greater than?" The honor challenges of the outside world are absent. Therefore, the socially acceptable contacts for the female disciples are expanded to include non-related males who are also disciples. Within the entire book of John, women are never placed exclusively inside a house. The public locations of the female characters are worth noting as a subversive gender construction.[33] They are out and about in public spaces contrary to expectations. Because Jesus meets Martha and Mary outside in public space, he is not reinforcing societal norms.

This section on how events, timing, and spaces are linked is only a sample of the artful way that the author has set together the entire book and especially the narratives under examination. All indications that the author offers in the narrative as repetitions of themes, the buildup of conflict, the scattering of motifs, and timing are pointing to the event of the cross ahead. The spaces and movement are becoming narrower and constricted so the vision of the reader is funneled to Jesus, "that you may believe." The next chapter includes general comments about the qualities of characters that inhabit the settings that have been created.

---

31. Brant, *Dialogue*, 218.

32. Neyrey, "What's Wrong with this Picture?" 114.

33. Yamaguchi, *Mary & Martha*, 177, n14.

7

The Writer Weaves the Narrative

CHARACTER DEVELOPMENT: THE PEOPLE WHO INHABIT THE SPACES

THE FOURTH GOSPEL WRITER chose to portray characters in a way that would provide the most convincing conveyance of the message. "Much of the power of the Fourth Gospel comes from its vivid characterizations and their effects upon the reader."[1] The characters of John are among the most memorable of the Gospels, yet they are only described with the absolute minimum necessary to support Jesus as main character. Details that would round out their characters such as age and appearance are not offered. The most revealing aspect about them is their speech, yet their manner of speaking is not peculiar to the individual, but they all speak in the style the author writes. One of the two main characters we are considering is Mary, who does not speak much at all, and not surprisingly, neither does Lazarus. Characters of ancient literature are often said to be "flat" compared to modern literary characters, who are more "rounded." More recently, this has been contested, and characters such as Mary and Martha are determined to be complex, developing, and rounded.[2]

1. Culpepper, *Anatomy*, 7.
2. Lee, "Characters and Characterization, 198." Lee is working with research on characterization by Cornelis Bennema.

Female Characters: The Women Are the Story

Because this book is focused on female characters, the depth and number of women characters is of particular interest. Both Luke and John appear to use pairs of men and women, but Beirne notes a difference between the two Gospels.[3] She says gender pairs in Luke seem to serve to emphasize the role of women or separate them as women into a group. In John, the women are actual characters that move the narrative forward. The man-woman pairs are not obviously side-by-side, but pairs can be discerned such as the Samaritan woman (4:1–26) with Nicodemus (3:1–15), and Mary of Bethany with Judas (12:1–11).[4] I particularly agree with Conway who finds that the gender choice of characters is an intentional aspect of Johannine characterization.[5] One effect of having both genders represented in the text reminds the reader that the faith and belief of Johannine discipleship belongs equally to all, women and men alike. An interesting question is the impact of the character's gender on the lesson being taught to the intended audience. Would the effectiveness of the character be as great if female characters were male and vice versa?

The deliberate movement of Jesus to associate with those of the socially lower strata is emphasized by his regular interactions with women. As mentioned in the honor/shame section above, Jesus constantly exemplifies a contrasting sense of honor as compared with the prevailing honor code, by including the disabled, the foreign, and women. If women had not been included in John, this potential for elevating all of the less honorable would have been minimized. Imagine if the sisters of Bethany had been brothers who were seeking to save the life of their sister, the story would have been less effective. It is an indication of the authenticity of the story that females were taking the initiative to take care of the male sibling, when normal patriarchal precedence would have portrayed the opposite.

The Jews: A Group Can Form a Character

In the section above, "the Jews" were discussed in their cultural-historic context, i.e., who they were, and the variety of people who were considered in that cultural group. In this section, they are considered in their various

3. Beirne, *Women and Men*, 25.

4. Beirne, *Women and Men*, 168.

5. Conway, *Men and Women*, 66.

roles as characters. The Jews are mentioned prominently in John 11–12 and appear to influence every event. The disciples worry about Jesus' safety as they attempt to dissuade Jesus from returning to Jerusalem because "they recently tried to stone him (11:8)." Ominously, Thomas points out that the Jews likewise threaten the lives of the disciples (11:16). Jews have come out from Jerusalem to comfort the grieving family, and they also report Jesus' actions back to the Pharisees in Jerusalem when they witness the event. Notably, some are said to "believe" (11:45).

As a group, they provide an interesting example of how a group can function collectively as a character. Therefore, the identity of the Jews as friend or foe and their relationship to the sisters is important to determine the role of Mary in encouraging the Jews to respond to Jesus. Interpretations of the Jews' roles within the Lazarus pericope vary widely. Schneiders claims the Jews play no essential role in the raising story itself although they do serve to "lace the story tightly into its Gospel context."[6] The Jews are portrayed positively and appear benignly, even compassionately in the household of Mary and Martha as fellow mourners in vv. 18, 31, and 33.[7] They follow Mary to meet Jesus, and witness the miracle (11: 45). Ambivalently, these same Jews, or others among them, go to tell the Pharisees of Jesus' actions (11: 45). Whether this is an example of spreading good news, or if they intended to get Jesus into trouble, is impossible to determine, but lines for and against Jesus are becoming firm. As a result, the authorities not only plot to kill Jesus (11:50), but also to put Lazarus to death (12:10). By John 12, the threat turns into a formal sentence on Jesus' life (v. 53). The Jews related the death of Lazarus to the previous healing of the man born blind in chapter 9, by noting in 11:37, "Could not he who healed the blind man have saved Lazarus?" The dispute with the Jerusalem Jews in chapter 10 is thereby brought into connection with the Lazarus miracle. Who among them will take a stand for belief in Jesus and who rejects him?

The leadership of "The Jews" becomes a monolithic character, one-dimensional, with a single trait: their unbelief in Jesus. According to Davies, the Jews and their leaders exemplify the unbelieving world in the Gospel story.[8] This is an example where the structure of a narrative takes on a dynamic of its own, irrespective of historical evidence. The Jews become a foil to enhance and accentuate Jesus' point of view, i.e., 7:35 and 8:22, where

6. Schneiders, "Death" 45.

7. O'Day and Hylen, *John*, 117.

8. M. Davies, *Rhetoric*, 300.

the Jews do not understand that they cannot go where Jesus is going, and in 10:24 where their unbelief is exposed when they wish for him to "speak plainly."[9] The crowds are impressed by Jesus without coming to full belief. "The Jews make concrete the world's hatred. They force believers to form their own community of mutual love." Yet there are those of the Jews who join with the Jesus followers.[10]

The conclusion for this thesis is that the leadership of the Jews is constantly influencing the proceedings of this pericope. Jesus' main interest is in bringing as many Jews to true belief and eternal life as possible. This occasion is the last open, public ministry to the Jews; it is important to determine their receptiveness. The death of Lazarus is the occasion to demonstrate his last sign. The Jews from Jerusalem came out to comfort the family, providing the audience, which Mary drew out of her house when she met her "teacher."

Conversation: Not Only the Words Are Important

Another aspect of the narrative structure of a text is the function, not the content, of conversation. Throughout the Fourth Gospel, but particularly as it progresses, the integration of the action of the story and the discourse become closely intertwined. Speech slows the action, action moves the speech, and they work together well, especially in the Lazarus narrative. As my perspective concerns conversation primarily between Jesus and women, the observations will be limited to that particular combination of discourse. Although conversations between women and Jesus are very limited in the Synoptics, in John a few examples are more extensive, such as the conversation with his mother (2:1–12), the Samaritan woman at the well (4:1–26), with Martha (11:17–27), and Mary Magdalene (20:11–18).

The understanding of a dialogue and the response to it depends on the setting, the individuals' status, and their relationship to each other, as well as the linguistic conventions that are ritualized in the cultural context.[11] Spencer finds that the commonality in women's conversations with Jesus is that they are trying to establish and maintain connection, intimacy, and

9. Resseguie, *Strange Gospel*, 129.

10. M. Davies, *Rhetoric*, 301.

11. D. Tannen's work from *Gender and Discourse* is quoted by Spencer, "You Just Don't Understand," 19.

community.[12] Martha's conversation with Jesus in John 11 is a good example of maintaining intimacy with Jesus.

Additional interesting qualities of discourse in John may be easy to miss if the reader is not aware of the details. The characters do not talk to each other; they mostly talk only to Jesus, especially in the passages under study.[13] The statement of Martha to Mary: "The teacher is asking for you," is actually unique. Typically, the men are ignoring, or talking over any women involved, as Judas who is talking over Mary to the men in attendance (12:4–5).

In the first half of this chapter, I have discussed the structural components of the texts as they are of interest to narrative criticism and particularly impact understanding of Mary and Martha. We reviewed awareness of how time, as manipulated by the author, can subtly indicate which points are most important. Movement between closed and open spaces and the use of the settings implicitly sends messages that may be easily missed if not pointed out. Character development and spoken lines often reveal much more than the content of the words. Narrative criticism brings new awareness of an additional layer of information from the text revealed in these structural features. Qualities of the texts under consideration come into clearer view if the reader takes careful notice of how discrete sections are related, and the development of the plot and conflict. More subtleties remain to be discovered in the figurative devices to be discussed in the last half of this chapter.

FIGURATIVE LANGUAGE INFLAMES UNDERSTANDING

The last section of this chapter describes the qualities of narrative criticism, and introduces terminology that will be used in chapter 8 when the results are applied to Luke 10:38–42 and John 11:1—12:11. The figurative language of the book of John is more challenging than what is found in the Synoptics, but rewarding to examine carefully.[14] Necessarily these brief paragraphs are only the essentials necessary for introduction to the figurative language of the Gospel as a whole. The boundaries of the categories are fluid and often overlap, but are worth study because they present particularly unique insights to the texts of Mary and Martha.

12. Spencer, "You Just Don't Understand," 45.

13. Culpepper, *Anatomy*, 145.

14. Brown, *Community*, 62.

Double Meanings: When Jesus Speaks—Listen Twice

Jesus frequently makes use of word plays and double meanings in a contest in which his opponents fall victim and he emerges the winner. Many statements are designed by Jesus to set others on the wrong course.[15] Jesus deftly manages to get his opponents to reveal their true character; they must decide if they are with him or against. The double meanings have more than one level of meaning, e.g., a literal and a symbolic. Examples are found in 3:21 when he speaks of the "temple as his body." In 12:23 Jesus speaks of a "seed that must die first in order to grow," an example he does not intend to be taken literally, but to describe the effect of his death. When Jesus speaks of "being lifted up" (8:28) or "being glorified" (12:23), he is speaking of his crucifixion, which would have become clear to his audience only after the fact.

Dialogue with Jesus is meant to challenge the Johannine reader to understand more than the characters, to be on the side of belief, and know Jesus more deeply. Often the narrator explains the meanings so the reader has the satisfaction, or discomfort, of knowing more than the Johannine characters.[16]

Foreshadowing: Hints of Things to Come

Examples of foreshadowing abound throughout John and more are discovered with each reading. Early in the book, the fate of John the Baptist already foreshadows Jesus' death (4:35).[17] The concentration of references to Jerusalem, e.g., 11:55, 56; 12:12, in the passages of this thesis alone, and the mention of approaching Passover, e.g., 11:55; 12:1, 20, ratchet up the sense of foreboding. Parallel to the increased references to approaching time and the nearness of Jerusalem, is the increasing clarity of the plot to kill Jesus, e.g., 11:57, 12:19. The remark of Caiaphas in 11:50 sends a foreboding shiver through the reader. Additional mention of the authorities' awareness of the growing popularity of Jesus, e.g., 12:10–19, 20–21, and detailing of Jesus' movements all pile on hints by means of foreshadowing.

By the time the reader has reached John 11 and 12, the reader has already, although perhaps unconsciously, read many hints of upcoming

15. Brant, *Dialogue and Drama*, 128.

16. Brown, *Community*, 62.

17. Beirne, *Women and Men*, 141.

events. The most obvious examples are the raising of Lazarus, which Jesus first anticipates in his conversation with Martha in 11:25, and then carries out physically (11:43). These acts all foreshadow the eventual resurrection of Jesus. Mary's anointing of the feet of Jesus prepared for his entry into Jerusalem as King of Israel (12:13) and victory over the prince of the world (12:31). The Mary and Martha pericopes are saturated with events that anticipate the crowning event of the resurrection at the conclusion of the Gospel.

Irony: Jesus' Sharp Tongue

The Fourth Gospel is particularly rich in the use of both subtle and obvious irony to convey effectively the message of the author. The study of irony in John greatly increases appreciation for the writing skill of the author. John's irony makes demands of the reader. More than any other literary device, it requires a shared sense of understanding and fellowship between the author and audience.[18]

Typically, the Fourth Gospel has characters make ironic statements that express a sensible meaning within the story. The narrator points out a broader significance and a more complex meaning. In this way, irony functions to distinguish between "insiders" and "outsiders."[19] The implied author of John is assuming the implied readers possess a certain amount of background knowledge. As they acquire understanding, the reader becomes more of an "insider." In order to appreciate the irony, the reader has to shift from the perspective of the character to that of the narrator.

Jesus often asks ironical questions which undermine the validity of implied claims. In 10:32, Jesus states a fact about his works and then discloses the incongruence of the resulting threat against him, "I have shown you many good works . . . for which of these do you stone me?" Irony requires that the reader be amused by the character's ignorance and should feel superior to it.[20] A selection of ironic items in chapter 11 include the statement of Thomas: "Let us also go, that we may die with him," (11:16). Little did he know that the disciples would desert Jesus at the cross (20:26). Martha confesses her belief in the "resurrection and the life" (11:27), but yet does not expect the revivification of her brother (11:39). In chapter 12,

---

18. Duke, *Irony in the Fourth Gospel*, 29.

19. Culpepper, *Anatomy*, 164.

20. M. Davies, *Rhetoric*, 365.

following the supper celebrating the life of Lazarus, his life is threatened (12:10). The man raised from the dead is threatened with death, and Jesus who brought Lazarus life, is condemned to death.

For the most part, irony surrounds the characters of Mary and Martha, they do not seem to be direct victims of Jesus' irony. Throughout the book, the absence of this prominent device in his interactions with the women says something; Jesus often seems to be gentler with those in the less privileged layers of society. Or, perhaps they just grasp the good news more quickly.

Misunderstanding as a Means to Understanding

The misunderstandings of the Johannine characters encourage readers to identify with the believing community while discerning the importance of Jesus, which the characters miss. The misunderstandings function to separate those who understand and believe in Jesus from those who do not. As readers understand, they become "insiders." "Misunderstandings are the writer's way to convince the believers to become believers, to reveal the readers to themselves, and to strip away their self-confidence."[21]

Culpepper observes three elements which characterize misunderstandings and the reaction of the reader: 1) Jesus makes a statement which is ambiguous, metaphorical, or contains a double-entendre. 2) His dialogue partner responds either in terms of the literal meaning of Jesus' statement, or by questions or protest, which shows that the person has missed the higher meaning of Jesus' words. 3) In most instances, Jesus or the narrator offers an explanation.[22] Two good examples occur in the John 11 passage. In 11:11–15 Jesus tells the disciples that Lazarus is "asleep," and in 11:23–25 Jesus tells Martha that her brother will "rise again." She assumes that he is talking about the general resurrection "on the last day." Martha experiences this (11:23) when Jesus says, "Your brother will rise again."

21. Brown, *Community*, 62.

22. Culpepper, *Anatomy*, 164.

Symbolism: Words Are More Than What They Seem

The Fourth Gospel is the most explicitly symbolic of all the Gospels.[23] Lee also points out that symbols in John are neither decorative nor arbitrary but substantial, part of the coherence of the good news."[24] Symbols require that in the act of reading, the reader must engage with other realities with outside information. The Greek word συμβάλλειν literally means "to put together," connecting links between the surface reality and a deep reality, but the connection is not identified in the text. The connection must be made from some other source as background knowledge, context, or culture.[25]

In the passages under study, the anointing of Jesus' feet is important in its own right and even more so because of the location in the center of the Gospel.[26] Koester understands Mary's anointing paired with Jesus' washing of the disciple's feet as both directing the readers' attention on the work and death of Jesus.[27] This action of Mary's could be a symbol of hospitality, honor, embalming for death, or consecration to kingship, each of which could be an appropriate interpretation. As illustrated in Mary's act, symbols rarely limit themselves to one meaning, and can move between several. The "fragrance that spreads through the house" (12:3) can likewise have a variety of meanings. The gift of ointment could be Mary's response to the gift of Lazarus's life given by Jesus and a proleptic response to the gift of the cross.[28] Mary herself could be a symbolic contrast of loving services as opposed to Judas, who brings death (12:4). Mary's importance in the narrative is emphasized by the numerous symbolic interpretations of her act (12:3). She is ultimately the symbol of the disciple's communion, and also the communion of all followers in love and abiding.[29]

Metaphors: Two Items Compared

Metaphors are a figure of speech created verbally either in oral or written literature. A metaphor is a specialized kind of symbol that draws a

---

23. Lee, *Flesh*, 16.

24. Lee, *Hallowed in Truth and Love*, 44–45.

25. Stibbe, *Storyteller*, 19, 27.

26. Lee, *Flesh and Glory*, 197.

27. Koester, *Symbolism*, 127.

28. Koester, *Symbolism*, 129.

29. Lee, *Flesh and Glory*, 210.

comparison between two different items that have one quality in common in the form of "A is B."[30] A good metaphor goes beyond merely dressing up the language, but actually improves on the reader's understanding of the concept. Examples of metaphors are the seven "I am" sayings in which Jesus declares who he is. The reader then must infer the similarity between the two items compared.[31] In John 11, one such example appears: "I am the resurrection and the life" (11:25) in his discussion with Martha. She does not really understand it though, because her answer does not directly affirm the "I am" statement. Keeping Mary and Martha in mind, Mary receives the most symbolic language, but Martha receives one of the seven "I am" metaphors.

Explanations: A Poke in the Ribs

The narrator of John 11:1—12:11 offers several "asides or footnotes," which are little inside explanations to the implied reader to smooth the way to understanding. The first example is at 11:2, which hints especially at the coming importance of Mary of Bethany, and reminds the readers of information they should already know. This explanation indicates the upcoming importance of the Mary character, but no clear conclusion about her importance is immediately given. When the text offers such hints to the readers, the narrator gains their confidence. He can be relied upon as a guide to be followed. His view is not partial or limited, and he gives readers just the kind of information that enables them to comprehend the sense of the narrative. "In accepting his guidance, readers are also seduced into accepting his world-view."[32]

Rhetoric: Let Me Convince You

Rhetoric is the means by which the author tries to persuade the reader to accept his/her point of view. The passages under consideration are using deliberative rhetoric because the writer is trying to persuade the reader concerning the expediency of a future action.[33] Each section of the Book of

30. Klein, et al., *Interpretation*, 307.
31. Culpepper, *Anatomy*, 181.
32. M. Davies, *Rhetoric*, 369.
33. Klein et al., *Interpretation*, 432.

John adds to the readers' understanding, so that by the end of the Gospel they are in a position to be convinced that Jesus is the Christ, the Son of God. The reader is constantly required to make connections with what precedes and follows. Questions must be asked as to what kind of remark this is: literal, ironical, metaphorical, theological, or philosophical.[34] Development is not so much in the story but in the readers. "By engaging in this exercise of comprehension, they are predisposed to accept rather than reject the Gospel's contentions."[35]

Applied to the Lazarus story, when Jesus and the disciples arrive in Bethany, Lazarus' death comes as a surprise, since Jesus had already told the disciples that Lazarus' illness "is not unto death; it is for God's honor." Therefore, Jesus' opportunity to maintain credibility is lost, and the assurance contradicted.[36] The narrator omits mention of any participants other than Jesus and Martha, who opens the conversation. Martha confirms the reader's impression that Jesus' presence would have saved Lazarus, as it had saved the royal official's son, the feeble cripple, the hungry crowds, the threatened disciples, and the man born blind, because "Jesus received whatever he asked" from God. But now that Lazarus is dead, what can Jesus ask? All that is left for them to ask of Jesus is that the sisters would be comforted in their distress. Jesus offers the comfort by reminding Martha that "her brother will rise again," and Martha responds by confirming her belief in the future resurrection. Jesus goes on to make a declaration about himself. He claims to be the "resurrection and the life." Martha's confession sums up the total truth of all teaching so far in the Gospel as Peter's did in the Synoptics. As she is convinced so should all readers, ancient and modern.

When Mary meets Jesus, she is accompanied by "the Jews." She falls at his feet and by her action presents a visual depiction of her confession. The Jews wonder whether what Martha and Mary had previously confessed could be true (11:37). Could Jesus have kept this man from dying? At the tomb, the reader must make connections with the earlier statements of Jesus. "Did I not tell you that if you would believe you would see God's honor? Also, "This illness is not unto death; it is for the honor of God." It leads readers into a more complete appreciation of Jesus' mission, but makes them wait until the last chapters for full comprehension.

34. M. Davies, *Rhetoric*, 112.

35. M. Davies, *Rhetoric*, 370.

36. M. Davies, *Rhetoric*, 371.

This concludes only a selection of the literary devices most prevalent in John 11:1—12:11. In addition to foreshadowing, irony, misunderstanding, metaphors, and rhetoric, many more could be discovered. When the figurative language is unraveled, the author teaches the reader how to understand the narratives. Readers learn that the literal meaning is not always what is intended, but that they must become initiated into a deeper meaning. The writer of John pulls the reader into the narrative in imaginative and ingenious ways, which teach the great truths of the Gospel while influencing with powerful and beautiful language. All literary devices are employed for the purpose of convincing the reader of the Gospel to accept Jesus as the divine revealer, and to share in the evangelist's concept of authentic faith.[37]

This chapter has briefly summarized many characteristics of a narrative directed by the author and interpreted by the reader. Recognition of these concepts and familiarity with terms is necessary for a thorough understanding of the narrative analysis, which follows in the next chapter. A new appreciation of the literary devices and narrative techniques used by the author of John greatly increases the interpretive possibilities of the Mary and Martha characters. Instead of a very simplistic understanding, these passages can reveal new complexity and interest.

37. Culpepper, *Anatomy*, 225.

PART III

8

The Portraits Come in Focus

Part II moved into the social-cultural background that brings alive the first-century world of Mary and Martha. I reviewed contextual and structural issues, as well as concepts of reader and writer that are necessary to appreciate nuances of the text. The author of John makes use of figurative language for especially original and vivid expression, which if noticed, adds much to the stories. In Part III, we will begin to see the results and summarize the various pieces of information gathered from all the study of both the Lukan and Johannine passages. Surprising connections will be made which form a whole new background to Mary and Martha. The new perspective comes into focus in this chapter. I will take you on a walk-through of all analysis done so far and the puzzle parts begin to come together to form new portraits of the sisters. Some items are briefly repeated from previous chapters to fully put the new information into context.

LUKE 10:38–42: NARRATIVE ANALYSIS

We start by going back to Luke to form a new continuous story. Luke 10:38 begins with no grammatical connection to the previous verses and indicates the start of a new narrative. Jesus and his companions are traveling around in an undisclosed location. The most recent mention of a place name is in 9:51, when he resolutely sets forth for Jerusalem. In 9:52 he is headed in the right direction when he sends messengers ahead into an unnamed Samaritan village. By 10:13, Jesus has made a U-turn when he proclaims "woe" on three villages on the north shore of the Sea of Galilee. Jesus appears to be diverted from movement south for several chapters. In 17:11, he is still on his way to Jerusalem. Chapter 19, he finally arrives in Jericho and enters Jerusalem in 19:28. According to this sequence, wherever Jesus may be in 10:38, the narrator has chosen not to reveal it. The possible location of Luke 10 as taking place in Galilee or east of the Jordan, was discussed above in chapter 4 of this book. Quite certainly, he is not in Bethany near Jerusalem at this point of his travels.

Looking at 10:38–42 narratively, I am particularly interested in where characters are located and moving, and who is talking and to whom. In 10:38 Jesus, apparently now alone, comes to an unnamed village and is received and/or greeted by a certain woman named Martha. Jesus approaches Martha as a grammatically singular person, so all other characters fall from view. Martha "received" Jesus, which may or may not indicate she received him as a guest in her house, but most importantly, she received his message. "In her (the) house" is not in the oldest Greek texts, and "kitchen" certainly is not. The main character, Martha, has a sister who also is known as "one who sits at the feet of Jesus," i.e., they have both spent time learning as disciples of Jesus. Both sisters are well-versed in the teachings of Jesus.

Martha is described as "pulled apart" by much unspecified service in verse 40. The reader is given no visual cues; the fly-on-the wall narrator does not say how one could know of Martha's distress. Apparently, Martha was not engaged in any activities that would betray her distress, e.g., she was not slamming pans around in the kitchen and working up a sweat. An observer would not know the source of Martha's worry or even if she was indeed overly worried unless there were subtle sighs or weeping. The meaning of *diakonia* was established in chapter 3 to hold many possible but unnamed service activities. Martha suddenly appeared to Jesus some unknown time after the description of her being distracted in verse 40a. In the last half of verse 40, "She appeared to him." The temporal connection between when Martha "receives" Jesus, and when she "appeared" to him with the request is unknown. Her preliminary greeting of him could have been a few minutes earlier, a day, or longer.

In this narrative, Jesus first approaches Martha, then Martha approaches Jesus. Who approaches whom indicates who is in need of something from the other person. The reason that Jesus first came to Martha in her village is unstated, thereby indicating it is not important for the reader to know. Maybe Jesus did need a place to lay his head, but the narrator does not say, so it is not an issue in the passage. Martha does have reason to approach Jesus; she wants his intervention. She says, "Lord, do you not care that my sister has left me alone to manage all the *diakonia?*" (10:40). Martha brings up the issue concerning her sister, not Jesus; and then, he replies, not to the issue she raised, but to Martha's worry. Why does she ask the question rhetorically? Has Jesus ever shown her that he does not care? Perhaps in the length of their friendship, however long it was at this point, Jesus has shown the intuitive (divine) ability to know her concerns. She wonders why it is not working on this occasion. It seems that the narrator has Jesus subtly forcing Martha to bring up the issue, even if Jesus already well knows what it is. And he probably does. Then she states her request to Jesus directly, "Therefore, tell her, that she may give me a hand" (my translation). Martha does not really tell Jesus what to convey to Mary, only "tell her" followed by the reason, which is "that she may help." The reader does not know what behavior Martha wants from Mary, only that her sister be able to lend a hand with unspecified *diakonia*.

Jesus uses her name as a double vocative, "Martha, Martha," (10:41) which shows great concern. Now Jesus names her real issue, which Martha either did not recognize about herself, or was repressing. Martha may think she needs help, but Jesus knows that serious worry is what is eating at her. By prolonging the interchange, the narrator allows both characters to be more complex and rounded. The reader knows that Jesus is deeply perceptive about Martha's many issues, and Martha realizes that Jesus does indeed care, more than she knew. The focus of the first part of his answer is on Martha, and her worries and turmoil, not on Mary. Jesus does not tell Martha what she is supposed to do about her worry, or that he will do something about it; the narrator allows her no comfort. Jesus' answer then focuses on Mary. She has made a "good choice" and it will not be taken away from her (10:42). Martha's only consolation is that Jesus is aware of her worry and cares. She is also assured that Mary is blessed by Jesus in her occupation. What is the "good" that Mary selected? The "good" that Mary has chosen is that she is following Jesus, her call as she heard it, in the missionary ministry with Jesus. Martha wishes her sister would abandon this "good" to be with her. Martha cares more about her "peace of mind" than her sister's risky *diakonia* for Jesus. Chapter 11:1 starts with, "And then it happened Jesus was praying in a certain place." Perhaps the modern reader should disregard the chapter division and keep reading to find Martha's comfort. Jesus is praying and one of his disciples asks him to teach them how to pray. Could it be that Luke is suggesting that one should pray and have faith in these situations instead of worrying?

In comparison to John, the text of Luke 10:38–42 does not contain as many literary devices. Narrative analysis of the Lukan passage is not as rich and complex as analysis of the John passage I am about to discuss, but nevertheless by noting exactly how statements are made, what is said and not said, in four verses new conclusions can be drawn about the sisters. I have observed that Martha has real worries that are far removed from fretting about how many dishes to serve. The sisters probably get along much better than popularly portrayed, and they do not provide positive and negative examples of how to serve Jesus. Petty bickering about who is performing hostess duties is absolutely not part of the scene. Martha has very understandable concerns about Mary and prevails upon Jesus to influence her (younger) sister to return home. Now new and more accurate information about the character of the sisters can be carried into John.

Once more I reiterate the conclusion noted at the end of chapter 3. Mary is not on the scene. She has no dialog, she does not respond to accusations. We do not see or hear her because she is not at home. The lesson is not about taking time for contemplation versus being too busy. Study is still important, but by this scene, both sisters have put in many hours at the feet of Jesus. In comparison to the Gospel of John, the text of Luke 10:38–42 does not contain as many literary devices. The authors of each Gospel are writing to different audiences and have different purposes, therefore their writing style is contrasting. The Lukan passage is also very brief, but nevertheless by noting exactly how statements are made, what is said and not said, this compact passage can yield new conclusions about the sisters.

JOHN CHAPTER 11:1—12:11: NARRATIVE ANALYSIS

A narrative approach to the Gospel of John exposes details of the last sign of Jesus that results in his friend's returning to life, but ironically sets into motion his own death. Before John 11, Jesus is in retreat "across the Jordan" (10:40) where John had baptized, and "many people believed in Jesus because of his miracles" (10:42). John 11:1 begins, "But a certain man." The narrative generates tension from the very first words. A normal equilibrium is never established until the end of the chapter, and then only partially, because Jesus is placed into even greater danger which ends on the cross. The dilemma, "a certain one is sick," is immediately evident. The assurance of Jesus' love for this person, "the one you love is ill," (11:3) creates immediate discomfort by his lack of follow-up action. The narrator builds tension by noting that Jesus does not immediately go to the aid of his friend, but waits two days before departing. This delay is an example of a motif throughout the entire Gospel when Jesus determines his own timing of events.[1] His ultimate purpose, which is to bring belief in himself, is not determined by human expectations. "The village of Mary and her sister Martha" (11:1), is remarkable in that Martha is identified in relationship to Mary. In the first two verses of the pericope, both Martha and Lazarus are identified according to their kinship relationship to Mary. Primacy appears initially to be given to Mary from the very first verse.

John 11:2 includes a literary device known as a *prolepsis*, or a "narrative intrusion" which appears to refer to an event that is yet to occur in the text: "This Mary whose brother Lazarus now lay sick, was the same one who poured perfume on the Lord and wiped his feet with her hair." This apparent bit of foreshadowing raises some major questions for the reader. The narrator provides a sort of poke in the ribs to make the readers aware that they should be engaged in this story because it concerns someone they apparently should already know. The note concerning Mary, an "aside" inserted by the narrator at this point, alerts the reader to a connection between two key events. Yet, in 11:2 only the fact of an anointing is stated, not the time, place, or her motivation. This literary gap forces first-time readers and those with no background, to speculate about the circumstances and significance of the anointing. At the very least, the remark sets the reader on notice that the character Mary is going to have prominence in the coming story. It also binds the section 11:1—12:11 together. Indeed, an *inclusio* is formed by the appearance of Mary at the beginning of chapter 11 and as the main character of 12:1–9.

The author presumes that John's readers knew the upcoming anointing act of Mary either by oral tradition or from an earlier written source. Yet, this is the first introduction of Lazarus of whom the author assumes no prior knowledge in his readers even though Lazarus is the object of Jesus' final and most memorable sign. A person being raised from the dead should be as memorable as any event imaginable! Surprisingly, the historic writer does not assume his implied readers are "insiders" concerning knowledge about the Lazarus event. I find it hard to believe that Mary's act of anointing, which is yet to be told another chapter later, was more well-known than the revivification event of her brother. How can the reader know of one event and not the other?

1. O'Day and Hylen, 117.

The Gospel of John was written perhaps two generations after the occurrence of Mary's anointing of Jesus. Why would the implied readers of the last quarter of the first century be expected to have previous knowledge of Mary of Bethany? One would first suppose that the anointing at the supper in honor of Jesus was so remarkable that it had been repeatedly retold in the decades after the event among the Christ-followers. They knew of this certain Mary and were expected to be eager for more information about her. Yet, it would seem reasonable that they would also already know Lazarus because he was an important guest reclining at the dinner after being brought again to life.

The commentaries have come up with various theories concerning this *prolepsis*. Several consider the remark to be an insertion by later editors.[2] A second possibility is that Mary is so well known by the act of her anointing, that she can be referred to even before the event is recorded.[3] This would also indicate that the Gospel was written to a community of believers who is already familiar with an anointing story. If the implied readers are assumed to know one or more stories of an anointing, at this point they are invited to recall these stories and make a connection. Now they may identify Mary of Bethany as the unnamed anointing woman in other Gospels, and add this to their background knowledge as they approach this story.

These same commentators often point out that even if the readers do not know the upcoming anointing narrative, it is a good literary device to draw special attention to Mary. O'Day and Hylen summarize this observation: "By pointing forward to the story of Mary's anointing of Jesus, the passion comes into view and begins to shape the reader's understanding of Lazarus's story."[4] A third possibility is that the author of John is assuming that his implied readers know of the story from reading the Synoptic narratives of Mark 14:3–9 and Matthew 26:6–13. This points out that although Mary of Bethany was not mentioned by name, now John is revealing her name, which was withheld in the Gospels that were written earlier.[5] In-

---

2. Brown, *Gospel*, 423, Schnackenburg, *Gospel*, 322; Lindars, *Gospel*, 386–387.

3. Examples that consider this possibility include Ridderbos, *Gospel*, 386; Mullins, *Gospel*, 262; Köstenberger, *John*, 326; Whitacre, *John*, 277; Morris, *Reflections*, 403; Beasley-Murrey, *John*, 185; Carson, *Gospel*, 407; Lincoln, *Gospel*, 318; Morris, *Expository*, 537; Bruce, *Gospel*, 239.

4. O'Day and Hylen, *John*, 113.

5. This possibility is considered by Burge, *John*, 312, n 5; Pink, *Exposition*, 158; Thomas, *Gospel*, 311;

deed in the Markan account Jesus said, "Wherever the Gospel is preached throughout the world, what she has done will also be told in memory of her" (Mark 14:9). It would be very disappointing if the name of the woman who should be so memorialized was forgotten. The fourth and last possibility is that the readers are familiar with the anointing woman of Luke 7:36–50. Yet the Lukan anointing event is quite different from the others. I will reveal my conclusion and its importance as the book progresses.

The sisters have sent the simple message in 11:3, "Lord, the one you love is sick." It would be surprising that Jesus must be reminded that this man is someone he loves. This remark is better explained as a narrative comment for the readers' benefit to heighten the tension and hasten Jesus' response. The sisters do not directly ask him to come immediately. They only state the fact and leave it to Jesus to decide what he will do. This is reminiscent of his mother's "non-request" in 2:3, "They have no more wine." In that culture, it is unusual that the sisters are taking the initiative in the care of the male member of the family contrary to the expected patriarchal family structures. An obvious question is how did the sisters know where Jesus was located? That they knew his whereabouts indicates a special insider's knowledge of Jesus' travel plans. Speculation about how this information was obtained is discussed in the geographical section above. My thoughts are that Mary and Martha were residing in their home "on the other side of the Jordan," until their brother's illness became critical and then they moved to Bethany to be near him.

Jesus assures his disciples in 11:4 that "this sickness will not end in death." Now the reader experiences emotional relief because surely Jesus knows the truth of the situation. This statement also anticipates the outcome of the story. The reader is told to expect a positive outcome.[6] The intended readers are relieved that the sisters will not lose their brother. This is confirmed when Jesus adds, "it is for God's glory that God's Son may be glorified through it." The narrator has set this up so the reader assumes this will be another healing miracle as Jesus was already performing on the other side of the Jordan in 10:40–42. In 11:5, the narrator informs the reader, "Jesus loved Martha and her sister and Lazarus." Now the status of Martha is raised by her mention while Mary is not named, so the status between the two is leveled. The omniscient narrator, knowing Jesus' thoughts, affirms the love that Jesus has for the family. The narrator takes care to underscore the close relationship between Jesus and these characters. The sisters' origi-

---

6. O'Day and Hylen, *John*, 113.

nal claim that "the one you love" is indeed supported. The reader trusts the narrator's factual judgment and gains confidence in the telling of the story.

The reader is surprised when informed in 11:6, "that Jesus stayed where he was two more days." This information sets up a dissonance because Jesus is assumed to care about those he loves and the reader experiences anxiety when Jesus does not show urgency to go to Bethany. The assurance of Jesus' love is in conflict with his inaction. This is reminiscent of other events that occur according to Jesus' time as in 2:4, to the royal official in chapter 4, and to his brothers in chapter 7:9–10, which is a recurring motif. Jesus' own sense of timing and his ultimate purpose are not determined by human time.[7]

When he does say that they should go back to Judea, tension is introduced by the disciples who remind him, "A short while ago the Jews tried to stone you, and yet you are going back there?" (11:8). Now the reader may understand Jesus' hesitancy in going to the sick one he loves. Is he worried about his own life? Another dilemma is set up; the readers ask whether Jesus will choose between the welfare of his friend or himself. When Jesus tells the disciples, "Our friend Lazarus has fallen asleep, but I am going there to awaken him" (11:11), the disciples comically take him at his word and reply, "Lord, if he has fallen asleep, he will be all right." The narrator must insert, "Now Jesus had spoken of his death, but they thought that he meant taking rest in sleep." This is an example of the often-used device, the Johannine misunderstanding. The narrator serves as interpreter of Jesus' words. These exchanges with the disciples are brief, and they do not develop into contests because the disciples seem to concede to Jesus' preeminence.[8] The disciples misunderstand and the narrator explains, "Then Jesus told them plainly, Lazarus is dead." The author presents the narrator as the one who understands Jesus' words when the disciples, as typically portrayed, do not.

The ambiguity is a confusion of the literal language with the figurative, an illustration of human misunderstanding of who Jesus really is. Jesus uses "sleep" figuratively to mean death while the disciples understand it literally. "For the disciples it was a temporary illness, to Jesus a temporary death!"[9] The disciples unwittingly state the truth when they say that Lazarus's sleep

---

7. O'Day and Hylen, *John*, 113.

8. Brant, *Dialogue*, 128.

9. Beasley-Murray, *John*, 187.

is a sleep "which leads to final salvation."[10] In this instance, without the narration, the dialogue loses its significance.[11]

After the disciples' confusion of whether Lazarus is "ill" or "asleep," in verses 11:12–13 Jesus states clearly that Lazarus is dead and the purpose of their going to him, "So that you may believe." The crowning theme is now introduced which will culminate at 11:42 in Jesus' prayer at the raising of Lazarus. Meanwhile, at every step of the way, the close associates of Jesus believe, then members of the crowd, and witnesses of the event are added as believers. Thomas stays true to character in his rash statement, "that we may die with him" (11:16). He continues to have his physical well-being foremost in mind instead of his belief, which is the concern of Jesus. In 11:17, the narrative time has been accelerated because suddenly four days have passed, if one considers that Lazarus died at the time Jesus said, "Let us go back to Judea."[12] No conversation or events are recorded during the time that Jesus and the disciples are traveling for one to four days.

The Scene Changes to Bethany

Upon arrival in Bethany, the reader reads with disappointment in 11:17: "Lazarus had already been in the tomb for four days." This is devastating because there is no possibility of a mistaken message. It may also raise confusion in the minds of the readers after Jesus' assurance in 11:4 that "the sickness would not result in death." Yet, the death is absolutely, unmistakably final. The location of Bethany is noted to be close to Jerusalem to explain the presence of many Jews. This geographical note also says something about the implied readers, i.e., that they were not familiar with the area of Jerusalem.

In 11:19, Martha receives the first literary mention: "Many Jews had come out to Martha and Mary." Although Martha is mentioned first in 11:19 and approaches first in 11:20, Mary was mentioned first in the opening of the pericope at 11:1 indicating that she was better known. When Martha heard that Jesus was approaching the village, she went out to meet him, but Mary stayed at home (11:20). Keener points out that sequence of names are not always an indication of significance to the story. It may be that Mary's

10. Resseguie, *Strange Gospel*, 47.

11. Culpepper, *Anatomy*, 34.

12. The distance traveled is calculated differently depending on when Lazarus died. Beasley-Murray has another interpretation p 188.

role in the narrative is second not because it is secondary, but because it is climatic.[13] The author appears to be keeping the sisters in a power balance.

The family had a large circle of friends or followers, although the reason for their prominence is not mentioned. When Jesus arrives on the outskirts of Bethany, perhaps he can already see or hear the commotion surrounding the residence of Martha and Mary from a distance. The extent and passion of mourning reflect the honor and esteem given Lazarus in the village. By referring to the nearness of Jerusalem (11:18), the text increases the reader's sense of Jesus' jeopardy when he arrives. Throughout this passage, the mere mention of Jerusalem is a motif of danger. His enemies in Jerusalem who wished to "stone" him, would certainly learn of his presence in Bethany, just over the Mount of Olives. He could not slip into Bethany incognito and comfort the sisters.[14]

Why does Jesus pause outside the village and does not immediately accompany Martha to the house? The emphasis early in the scene is on the presence of many Jews who had come to Martha and Mary. It is not at all clear, as one representative commentary states: "The Jews in this story are clearly positively portrayed, as they support Mary and Martha in their grief and weep with the sisters."[15] Perhaps Jesus was intentionally delaying the time when he would face the Jews who were an unknown entity to him, e.g., were they friendly or antagonistic? Remember the probability discussed in chapter 5, that Jews could simply be a reference to Judeans, i.e., friendly or neutral inhabitants of Judea and Jerusalem. Or, they could have less amicable purposes toward Jesus. They could be loyal to the family, but not necessarily to Jesus. Perhaps he wanted to meet them in a neutral public or open space instead of inside a closed house, or he preferred to delay word of his arrival reaching Jerusalem where the Jewish authorities would be notified. "As is evident from Martha's private communication to Mary, what mattered to Jesus above all was contact with his beloved friends."[16] Perhaps he needs them as much as they need him. It is Jesus' last pause before the irreversible momentum to the cross.

The cultural-historical background I reviewed earlier informs that according to Jewish custom relatives of the deceased are said to sit *shiva*

---

13. Keener, *John*, 845.
14. Burge, *John*, 316.
15. O'Day and Hylen, *John*, 117.
16. Ridderbos, *Gospel*, 400.

for a week following a death.[17] Mary apparently was reluctant to break this tradition, but Martha did not hesitate. Why does Martha greet him outside the village when she could have waited for Jesus to approach the house? A servant could have shown him the way if that was necessary. From Martha's point of view, it seems she must have found the condolences that were being offered in the house by the Jews from Jerusalem to be not very comforting. Maybe they were Mary's friends, but not particularly hers. She would rather see Jesus, and made this effort to catch him alone before he was swamped by the crowd. We have always thought of Martha as being the "social" sister, and Mary the "loner," but maybe this was a preconception from a false impression of the Lukan passage.

Looking at this from a narrative critical perspective, one makes particular note of the movements of characters across the landscape. "When Martha heard that Jesus was coming, she went out to meet him" (11:20). How is it that Martha was able to leave the house without attracting attention to herself? She slipped out either without anyone noticing or caring about her activity. On the other hand, when Mary leaves the house, "The Jews who had been with Mary consoling her, noticed the haste with which she got up and left, and they all followed her *en masse*, supposing she was going to the tomb to mourn" (11:31). A detail that caught my attention early in my research is the curious reason the visitors from Jerusalem kept a more watchful eye on Mary than Martha. Mary seems to have an entourage around her, but Martha appears to get as much attention as wallpaper. In my subsequent research, I eventually found only one older commentary that noted this detail.[18] This realization set me forth on a quest to determine the mystery of Mary. Why does she warrant this adoration, sympathy, and attention, but Martha seems to be overlooked?

Martha and Mary Meet Jesus

Martha takes prominence by demonstrating the presence of mind to carry on a conversation with Jesus as compared to Mary, who after repetition of the same initial statement of Martha, is overwhelmed with emotion. Martha asks Jesus obliquely for a miracle (11:22), which she believes could be possible if Jesus wills it. In her prior experiences with Jesus, she knows and

17. Keener, *John*, 842. The Jews mourned for seven days by sitting *shiva* at their house while receiving condolences from friends and relatives.

18. Pink, *John*, 196.

has witnessed that whatever Jesus asks from the Father, he receives. Because of his delay in arriving, she may doubt Jesus' willingness to do this for her. Apparently, neither of the sisters considered the possibility that Jesus could have also healed their brother from afar, as had occurred in the healing of the official's son (4:43–54). Jesus affirms in the following chapters of John that he always was with them, and always will be. They should trust him in his absence as when he is physically present.[19] This is also a reminder of a returning motif of "abiding" after belief which Jesus will emphasize in John 15.

In the dramatic world, it is worth noting the names a character is given by other characters, which indicates their standing and individuality. When Jesus proclaims, "I am the resurrection and the life" (11:25), he is referring to his resurrection as the promise of all human resurrection. In contrast, Martha proclaims him as "the one who was to come" (11:27). Jesus is saying he is the promised Messiah, guaranteeing he is the one he says he is. Characters, Martha included, persistently try to orient Jesus to their world, whereas Jesus removes himself from their world.[20] Martha states her understanding of Jesus, but Jesus corrects and refines it. Jesus always stays out of reach of human comprehension; in addition, the more he states his distinctiveness, the more resistance he experiences. A major theme in John is the identity of Jesus as the Christ and Son of God.[21] Christology is revealed through narrative strategies such as the "I am" metaphors.[22] The more that Jesus clarifies his identity, the more attention he draws, and those around him distance themselves from him.[23] This increasing revelation distances him from a recognizable name, and his listeners are antagonized; the division between believers and unbelievers increases.

In narratives of Jesus' miracles, the miracle is usually performed first, before the explanation. In this case, the explanation comes first. Therefore, Martha's confession concerning Jesus as the Christ in no way comes as a result of seeing the raising of Lazarus. Her confession is purely the response of Jesus revealing himself verbally as the "resurrection and the life." Martha

---

19. Schneiders, "Death," 51.

20. Brant, 171.

21. Köstenberger, *John*, 9 John's overarching purpose is the demonstration that the Christ, the Son of God, is Jesus."; Beasley-Murray, *John*, lxxxi, "The Theme of the Fourth Gospel is Christ"; Keener, *The Gospel*, 280, "Christology is central to this Gospel."

22. Tovey, *Narrative Art*, 99.

23. Brant, *Dialogue*, 170.

does not demand a sign.[24] "Time" as a motif appears again; Jesus determined the time the conversation turned to Mary, because the text (11:28) states that Jesus asked Martha to call Mary to come to him. "Calling" is also a motif in John; Jesus asked for Mary as he calls his "sheep" (10:3). At this time Jesus set into motion the actual performing of the miracle. Because the Jews followed her out of the house, the scene was set to go on to the tomb of Lazarus, and then finally on to Jesus' tomb. Note that between the sisters, they refer to Jesus as "the teacher." They had both spent time with him as students, and the fact they are women is not even particularly notable. This is further confirmation of a conclusion drawn from the study of Luke 10, that both Mary and Martha were students of Jesus, not just Mary.

"Quickly" is used twice in 11:29–31. Mary got up "quickly" to go to him and the Jews with her noticed when she "quickly" arose. The haste and eagerness with which she yearned to see Jesus is emphasized. In narrative criticism, the critic notices the frequency with which a character is noted. Yamaguchi points out that in the space of these few verses, an unusual concentration of Mary's name or feminine pronouns occurs that draws special attention to her relationship with the Jews.[25] "They had come to **Mary** and Martha" (11:19). "And after she had said this, she went back and called her sister **Mary** aside. The Teacher is here, she said, and is asking for **you** (28). When **Mary** heard this, **she** got up quickly (29). When the Jews who had been with **Mary** in the house, comforting **her**, noticed how quickly **she** got up and went out, they followed **her**, supposing **she** was going to the tomb to mourn there (31). When **Mary** reached the place where Jesus was and saw him, **she** fell at his feet (32). When Jesus saw **her** weeping, and the Jews who had come along with **her** also weeping he was deeply moved in spirit (33)." These many pairings of Mary with the Jews indicate a connection between the two, an important detail I will pick up on later.

It is remarkable that both sisters spontaneously, and independently, make the same remark upon meeting Jesus (11:21 and 32). Each sister individually recognizes Jesus for who he is and what he can do. Many different opinions have been ventured concerning the interpretation of the sisters' identical remarks upon meeting Jesus, "Lord, if you had been here, my brother would not have died." One could imagine that the conversation in the house between those consoling Mary and Martha was dominated by the question: "Where is Jesus?" "If he had healed the man born blind,

24. Schneiders, *Written That You May Believe*, 106.

25. Yamaguchi, *Mary & Martha*, 117.

then surely he could have healed Lazarus." Possibly this confidence-eroding conversation was being echoed in the house by the fellow-mourners from Jerusalem (11:37). It is possible that this line of thought was echoing in the sisters' minds and is first to their lips as each approached Jesus. Especially intriguing is the point that the writer is trying to make by having the narrator frame the sisters' approach with this particular remark repeated twice. A conclusion concerning the likely double function of the sisters' greeting to Jesus will be proposed in the following chapter of this book.

The scene of mourning over Lazarus in verse 32 contains elements of danger for Jesus. Readers sensitive to the categories of honor and shame,[26] notice the challenge to Jesus' honor posed by Mary's public allegation that Jesus could have done something to prevent her brother's death.[27] This may seem to charge Jesus with failure because Jesus has defaulted on his obligations as both Lord and friend.[28] Jesus is seen to disregard his own honor more frequently as he approaches the crucifixion.

Mary Cries, the Jews Cry, Jesus Cries

The possible meaning of Jesus' "crying" (11:35) has been discussed above in the Greek vocabulary section. From the description in the text, the narrator gives no hint as to the reason that Jesus demonstrates intense emotional distress or anger. It has already been established that "weeping" is too weak a translation. The Jews' comment, "See how he loved him," may or may not be an accurate commentary for the grounds of Jesus' tears. It may be a statement of their superficiality, because that is an easy assumption, but it could be the true source of his tears. Jesus' weeping may also signify a border crossing. Tears were a gendered category. Although men wept, tears were particularly characteristic of women. The Jews' reasonable explanation for Jesus' weeping does not necessarily undo the suggestion that Jesus acts like a woman.[29]

I am concluding that Jesus "bellowed out an enormous shudder," remarkable enough to capture notice with unusual vocabulary. Many proposals have been considered concerning the cause of Jesus' strong outburst of emotion. I suggest Jesus was crushed that the Jews following Mary did not

26. Malina, *New Testament World*, 33.

27. Brant, *Dialogue*, 214.

28. Spencer, "You Just Don't," 37.

29. Brant, *Dialogue*, 215.

also fall to their knees and worship him as God as Mary demonstrated. They were absorbed in their personal grief and failed to demonstrate belief that he is the resurrection and the life. The enormity of the crowd of lost people, devoid of real hope, bolstered his determination to perform the miracle and demonstrate the glory of God. Further, his strength was reinforced to continue the path to the cross and conquer death for all people who believe. I was particularly intrigued with the observation in verse 33 that Jesus made special notice of Mary's crying. Could it be that Mary's weeping brings to Jesus' mind a poignant memory? This is a tentative connection; a hint of the direction I will pursue below.

As the tomb comes more sharply into focus in verse 38, the emotional description continues to grow. The narrator carefully describes the emotions of Mary, the crowd, and finally Jesus. The sepulcher appears to be the occasion for the most unusual outpouring of emotions. The inner part of the narrative (11:17–44), which takes place within a single day, goes into the inner recesses of the women's belief system and forms a new conceptual framework.[30] The main characters are deeply involved. Spencer says it well: "They will remember not only the miraculous resurrection, but also the putrid fumes of his decomposition. Jesus' nostrils snort in anger, sniffle with weeping, and smell the stench of death."[31]

Jesus asks, "Didn't I tell you that if you believe, you will see the glory of God?" (11:40). The Gospel reader will pause here and ask, "What did I miss?" Originally, Jesus did not say this to the people in Bethany, but to the disciples upon hearing the news of Lazarus (11:4), and Martha was not there. Michaels presents a solution that the messenger, who brought the news from the sisters to Jesus on the "other side of the Jordan," that Lazarus was ill, returned to the sisters with these words from Jesus.[32] How much more disappointed they must have been when Lazarus died, if Jesus had indeed sent them reassurance: "This sickness will not end in death. No, it is for God's glory so that God's Son may be glorified through it" (11:4). As tenuous as that possibility is, no one has ventured an idea on how the sisters reacted when Lazarus died, despite Jesus' message that Lazarus' sickness will not end in death. Like the disciples earlier, the people in Bethany were supposed to get Jesus' double meaning concerning death. To Jesus it is only a "sleep."

30. Resseguie, *Strange Gospel*, 89.

31. Spencer, "You Just Don't Understand," 40.

32. Michaels, *John*, NIBC , 206.

Another explanation is offered by Douglas Estes concerning Jesus' question, "Did I not say?" (11:40) He says that Jesus did not intend a literal answer referring to a specific time and place.[33] Jesus phrased the negative question in such a way to elicit from Martha a strong affirmation. The conditional "if you believe," is the suggestion of possibility instead of a statement of fact. He is pleading with Martha, and all observers, to listen and believe right then and there! Estes points out how understanding the question of Jesus in this way places the climax of the chapter on this question, "If only you would believe." This is the plea to all readers of John in 11:25; 26; 40, and 42.[34]

Following immediately after the revivification of Lazarus, I noticed a text that appears inadvertently to omit the mention of Martha. Such is how the few commentaries that actually notice the omission seem to understand it. In 11:45 is the offhand remark, "Therefore many of the Jews who had come to visit Mary, and had seen what Jesus did, put their faith in him." Only one commentary ventures a reason for Mary's solo notice: "It may be that Mary is the only one mentioned because she was better known among John's readers."[35] He goes on to give the reason that perhaps "she was more emotional, and therefore not as resilient as Martha and thus was more in need of help from others."[36] The few words, "who had come to visit Mary" could have been omitted with no loss to the sentence. The end result is that many of the Jews, who saw Jesus' sign, became believers. Another of the big questions that originally caught my attention again concerns special attention given to Mary. Why is Mary singularly mentioned in this context? Who is she, that the Jews came out from Jerusalem to console her, but Martha is not mentioned? The mystery will continue.

The delay of the *parousia,* and the fate of Christians who die before the second coming of Christ, is a continuing theme in the New Testament as in Matthew 24–25, I Thessalonians 4:13–17, and Revelation 6:10, 14:13. The raising of Lazarus should not be considered primarily as a favor to the grieving sisters, but as Jesus' culminating self-revelation on the eve of his passion.[37] Martha's remark, "by this time there is a bad odor, for he has been there for four days" (Jn 11:39), is often taken to show her lack of faith, but

---

33. Estes, *The Questions of Jesus,* 156–57.

34. Estes, *The Questions of Jesus,* 157.

35. Morris, *Expository Reflections,* 419.

36. Morris, *Expository Reflections,* 419.

37. Schneiders, "Death," 48.

is a narrative confirmation to the onlookers, and subsequent readers, that Lazarus really was dead and starting to decay. She had no way of knowing or anticipating that at that moment Lazarus would be brought back to life. Her function at this time is to reinforce the reality that her brother was certainly dead—as dead as could be.

Narrative Results of John 12

Moving to chapter 12, the narrator identifies a passage of time in anticipation of Jesus' final Passover. Jesus is again in Bethany after an unspecified time since the last events. The narrator reminds the readers of the importance of the Lazarus sign, but the dinner is in Jesus' honor (12:1–2). Martha is the second sibling mentioned, she is performing *diakonia*, and she will not be noted again. Her possible exact serving activity was discussed above in chapter 3. In verse 3, Mary gets the next mention, and she will be the center of attention throughout.

A verbal motif occurs between the verb "to wipe" in John 12, which is the same verb used to describe Jesus' wiping of his disciples' feet at the footwashing in John 13:5. Mary's anointing and wiping of Jesus' feet, based on this one verb, could thus point toward Jesus' footwashing at the Passover feast. More sensory stimuli are brought in by the description of the perfume that permeated the house and overcame the memory of the stench of death from 11:39. Note that in the climax of both chapters 11 and 12, the author brings in the assertive voice of Jesus' commands: "Lazarus come out," and "Leave her alone," and the contrasting odors of either death, or fragrance of perfume. Mary's conduct comes under attack by Judas. Verse 4 paints a striking contrast in characterization between Mary and Judas, similar to the contrast between Mary and the unbelieving Jews in 11:37. Beirne points out: "In every sense, Mary represents the exaltation, and Judas the darkness of Jesus' death on the cross as anticipated by the evangelist throughout chapter 12."[38] The characterization of Judas is darkened so that Mary is lighter in comparison. The effect is like a spotlight shining on Mary as if she is on a stage. She is the centerpiece example of an adoring, grateful, serving disciple. The narrator gives no indication of her inner motivation, and there is no way of discerning if she really understands the prophetic sense of her deed. What we know about Mary's act is only known by means

---

38. Beirne, *Women and Men*, 141.

of the narrator's observation and Jesus' remark. Likewise, only the narrator gives us the truth about Judas, which will come out in chapter 13.

Here is another example of the narrator inserting an "aside" explaining Judas' ulterior motive as wishing the funds for himself and foreshadowing his role in 13:2. Narratively, this serves to portray Judas in an even darker light because not only does he indignantly object, but he hypocritically has his own devious motives. I love a quote I found in Ridderbos that I share here: "Outside the house in Bethany, shadows fell at the end of a day when the Son of God dwelt gloriously among humans at a banquet where he received such love."[39] Now the twelve hours of light are over, and darkness has crept in even within the group (cf. 9:4–5).

Looking ahead to John 13, Jesus crosses boundaries into the realm of shame by washing feet. Explored in the cultural section in chapter 5, washing of feet was done by the most menial servants in the house. Jesus willingly assumes that position. Peter's resistance to having Jesus wash his feet signifies his reception of the act as shameful to himself, or Jesus, or to both of them. At the Johannine Passover supper, Jesus anticipates the reversal of the categories of honor and shame at the crucifixion.[40] Mary, and Martha by her hospitality, played significant parts in foreshadowing this scene and setting the first example.

NARRATIVE CONCLUSIONS

The conclusions from narrative critical observations invite a new look at the pericopes and suggest new insights. Specifically, Mary of Bethany acquires a new portrait in Luke if she is taken out of the house and into an active ministry of her own. Martha is no longer the sister primarily concerned with social obligations and superficial concerns. No longer does this story look like a silly disagreement between the two sisters that they should have solved on their own. Prevailing upon Jesus to adjudicate an issue concerning housework makes the women look petty. If instead, Martha is worried about Mary being on the "mission field" with Jesus, then all who have felt abandoned by a loved one who goes away from home to do the Lord's work can empathize. This is a real concern for every family in this position.

The sisters are no longer in competition with each other, with one as the example of "better" and the other "lesser." They both have their

---

39. Ridderbos, *The Gospel*, 415.

40. Brant, *Dialogue*, 216.

appropriate ministries, one "away," and one in the village. Evidence is abundant that both sisters are learners at the feet of Jesus. Extraordinarily, this is a story with women as the main characters, and Mary is given permission by Jesus to be away from the traditional ministry for women. Martha is given permission to let go of her concerns about her sister and trust Jesus when her sister is absent. With these new insights, when the reader meets these characters again in the Johannine passages, a different background informs the situation.

Most importantly, instead of looking for ways to elevate one sister above the other, I find that the sisters meet Jesus separately, one privately and one publicly. One is not a "good example" or the other a "bad example." A couple loose ends appear after a close narrative analysis. I remarked that Martha was able to leave the house to see Jesus without attracting any attention. No one seemed to notice or care about her activities. Yet when Mary leaves the house, everyone gets up and speculates about her motive. Another mystery is the reason for Mary's sole mention in 11:45: that many Jews came from Jerusalem to console Mary, but Martha is not mentioned. Mary also receives extra mention in relationship to the Jews and other grammatical priority. The most important narrative results from analysis of John 11:1—12:11 include uncovering a mystery but no answer. What is the source of Mary's unexplained popularity?

9

Four Women or One?

ONE MAY BE EXCUSED for thinking that enough new information has been gleaned from a close look at Luke 10:38–42 and John 11:1—12:11. Are more secrets to be divulged by scrutinizing yet more texts? And we thought we knew Mary and Martha! This is quite enough newness to process so can there really be more to discover?

Careful study of Mary's anointing of Jesus in John 12:1–11 in comparison to the other "anointing stories," may not seem essential to my premise that the source of Martha's worry is the absence of her sister. Indeed, it is not essential; in Luke, Mary could be absent from Martha for any number of reasons, and with that information alone, the narratives of Mary and Martha in both Luke and John could have totally changed focus. However, I think there is more to discover. If the anointing woman of each Gospel version is the same Mary of Bethany we are researching, some surprising conclusions may uncover even a more complete portrait.

THE RELATIONSHIP OF THE VARIOUS "WOMEN WHO ANOINT"

Is it possible to recover a prehistory that occurred before the events usually associated with Mary and Martha? In John 11, a relationship of unusual closeness is clearly indicated, but the origin of their friendship is left unknown. I already established that both Mary and Martha had a previous relationship with Jesus as disciples learning at his feet before the scene of Luke 10:38, which was not Martha's initial meeting with Jesus. Can digging deeper into the "anointing stories" provide a possible prelude that expands Mary and Martha's prior relationship with Jesus?

Redaction Criticism

Redaction criticism as applied to the Gospel of John 11:1—12:11 investigates why the evangelist made the selection of this pericope, and presented it in the particular final form.[1] Redaction criticism also attempts to sift out the personal agendas or theological interests of the biblical authors by analyzing carefully the writing techniques, editorializing, interpretations, and especially the choices they made in the original material that they utilized in the finished text.[2] Horizontal comparison is made with parallel passages, which is not possible in study of Luke 10:38–42 and John 11 because there are no parallels to these pericopes in the other Gospels. On the other hand, an "anointing story" is featured in each Gospel, therefore comparison of the variations and similarities is possible and yields interesting information.

A complementary work of criticism is accomplished by reading vertically within the text of one author, and analyzing the progress of the complete work, or taking a smaller segment and looking for indications of greater importance placed on certain material. This can be seen by repetitions, form, and the order of material as it is introduced, summarized, or given special attention.[3] Following the dining scene in Bethany of John 12, and Jesus' washing the feet of the disciples immediately following in John 13, fall within vertical redaction.

A horizontal redactional comparison will be applied to the four "anointing" pericopes with a view towards concluding who is the main actor, at what location, and when in Jesus' ministry the incident(s) occurred. Another look at Mary's role in the one and perhaps more "anointing stories," may be fruitful because of the possibility that the parallel passages all describe a scene, or scenes, in which she was front, center stage.

All four Gospel writers considered a story of a woman anointing Jesus to be important theological material for their individual texts. How does one account for the variations and similarities between Matthew 26:6–13, Mark 14:1–9, Luke 7:36–50, and John 12:1–11?[4] Comparisons of the pas-

1. See also Blomberg, *Jesus and the Gospels,* 405.

2. Osborn, "Redaction Criticism" 128–149.

3. Fee and Stuart, *How to Read the Bible,* 135–143.

4. For charts summarizing the four anointing pericopes, see Getty-Sullivan, *Women*

sages made by commentators from a generation ago tend to harmonize the differences.[5] Evidence of attempts at harmonization goes back as far as Origin, although he refuted the conflation of the four pericopes. The story line is similar in each event, much vocabulary is repeated, and Jesus delivers the final line of approval. A sense of drama is built up because the reader tries to anticipate Jesus' reaction, that is, will he approve or reprimand the woman? Jesus admonishes the observers and explains the reason that the woman's deed is to be accepted and not condemned.

The appearance of common vocabulary indicates complex relationships between the four passages. The otherwise unique phrase λιτραν μύρου νάρδου πιστικῆς "pound-ointment-nard-pure" occurs only in John 12:3 and in the parallel passage of Mark 14:3.[6] The Johannine pericope has the most similarity with the Markan passage in three distinct details: as a pound of costly ointment of pure nard; sold for three hundred *denarii*; and Jesus' rebuke to the men, "Leave her alone." Because the striking vocabulary exactly coincides, it is possible that John used the story from Mark as a source or he had access to the same traditions that Mark also used. Another possibility is that the oral or written source of John was an eyewitness as the writer claims (21:24), but wrote it much later as discussed above.

Two different passages, twice in John 12 and three times in Luke, emphasize the word πόδας, and both use the verb "to anoint." These are small hints that the author of John drew at least minimally from Mark and Luke, though the argument could be made that such a unique vocabulary was transmitted orally. Other parallels exist among Matthew, Mark, and Luke, but not John, such as taking place at a house of someone named "Simon" and an "alabaster jar." Further, Bethany is mentioned in all accounts but Luke.

To summarize, vocabulary links are found between John and Luke concerning the perfume used. A three-way relationship between the two Johannine (chapters 12 and 13) narratives and the Lukan passage is convincing because of common vocabulary "feet" and "wiping." Yet, more three-way links are found between Matthew and the others. The overlap in the telling of the details coincides in numerous and complex relationships

---

in the New Testament, 107; Vinson, *Luke*, 228.

5. Lee, *Flesh and Glory*, 198. Also see the discussion, 167, n3.

6. Esler and Piper, *Lazarus, Mary and Martha*, 165–177. In an appendix, these authors study the textual history of this phrase and conclude that scribes of John in P 66 harmonized with the text of Mark.

in a way that no one story can be separated from the others on basis that it is more unique. Details are different but usually coincide between two or three of the narratives. The similarities are too great to make these three or four different events.[7] Therefore, on basis of vocabulary, for my study of the anointing scenes, initially, I conclude that these all refer to the same one or two events, not three or four. A strong link between Luke and John 12 is intriguing, yet the difference of time between the early part of Jesus' ministry and the location far from Jerusalem presents obstacles too large to explain away.

A SINNER IN THE CITY

Which writer was closest to the original event(s)? Two commentators who argue for the priority of John are Dodd[8] and more recently Coakley, who agree that the John 12 account depends on eyewitness memory.[9] I particularly agree with this stance because John seems to have details that the other accounts do not reveal. Mark and Matthew, who wrote an "anointing story" prior to the writer of John, either did not have all the details, or redacted it to their purposes. Another interesting, and very likely possibility is that Mark and Matthew purposely changed details to protect the safety of the characters still living.[10] By the time John was written, either the Bethany family members were no longer living, or they were out of danger. According to the above information, priority could be given to John on basis of being an eye-witness account, although recorded many years after the other Gospels were written.

I turn next to an analysis of the events as recorded, to explore the possibility that each text uses the one same historical event as a source. The script of events is similar in all four retellings. Jesus reclines at dinner with a group of men. An uninvited woman enters the room carrying container of perfumed ointment. Without a word she interrupts the dinner, anoints

7. J. Lyle Story, "Female and Male in Four Anointing Stories," 16–23. He states for the sake of his article, there were two original versions of the stories 1) Matthew, Mark, and John, and 2) Luke, in their oral transmission. He does not comment on the possibility of two original events. His article includes an extensive summary chart.

8. Dodd, *Historical*, 163–174. See for an extensive discussion and a chart.

9. J. F. Coakley, "The Anointing at Bethany and the Priority of John," 242.

10. Theissen, *The Gospels in Context*, 186–188. Because the characters of John 11 were in danger from authorities, this story was omitted in the earlier Gospels. By the writing of John, they were out of danger or deceased.

Jesus, other guests object, but Jesus approves. The variations in each text reflect divergent theological interests of the Gospel writers, which could account for some but not all the differences. A case could be made for four versions of the same event if one can accept heavy redaction, from Luke in particular.

One possible piece of supporting evidence that the pericopes derive from the same origin is that the host in both John and Luke is named Simon. This may seem like too big of a coincidence if these are not recording the same event, but Simon was the most common masculine name of the time. In addition, Simon the Pharisee in Luke 7 could not possibly be the same as Simon the Leper of Matthew 26:6 and Mark 14:3, because Pharisees would not have any contact with the unclean. A man suffering from leprosy would not be a Pharisee, therefore, intertextual crossover between these characters is unlikely.

A difficulty with the last conclusion is the location of Luke's pericope, both in the chronology of Jesus' ministry and the geographic location. In Luke 7:11, Jesus is in Nain (Galilee); the anointing by a "sinful woman" in 7:36 is at an undisclosed location. By 8:22, he is at the Sea of Galilee, and in 8:26, he sails to Gerasenes. No mention is made of any location near Jerusalem.

Analysis of the redactional interests of each Gospel writer determines that the theological purpose behind the stories shows differences that may further sort out the events. The greatest theological contrast is between Luke and the other three Gospels. Luke records the event as a lesson on forgiveness when Simon emphasizes her history of sin.[11] The unnamed woman expresses extreme sorrow with abundant tears, which wet his feet. Jesus compares the woman's reception and Simon's, who has neglected the tasks of a host, and then adds a parable of the two debtors inserted in verses 41–43.[12] John's contrasting theological concern is anointing, which fits the kingship theme of the Johannine passion narrative.[13] Mary's anointing of the feet instead of the head illustrates a different sort of kingship. She is anticipating the day of his burial. Kingship in John is all about service, which Mary of Bethany recognizes, but is entirely lost on Judas.[14]

11. Getty-Sullivan, *Women in the New Testament*, 105–113.

12. Coakley, "The Anointing," 256.

13. Beasley-Murray, *John*, 208.

14. Beirne, *Women and Men*, 168.

A few commentators argue for four variations of one original event.[15] Several commentators have proposed two different strands of tradition, if not two different events. Some determine it is impossible to untangle the origins.[16] More common is the conclusion that two different events took place.[17] John, Mark, and Matthew record an event shortly before Passion Week where Mary of Bethany is the female actor. Luke records an event known only from his unique material that occurred earlier in Jesus' ministry performed by an unknown woman. So far, I am tentatively concluding that intertextual comparison across the four Gospels indicates the four anointing pericopes originate with two different events. It is intriguing that some commentators note a similarity between the versions of Luke and John, e.g., anointing of feet rather than head, and wiping feet with hair.[18] Yet, they find the similarities do not overcome the differences between the Lukan and the Bethany anointings. I propose a reason for the intuitive connection that some commentators notice, yet cannot quite find convincing.

I am concluding at this point that Mary of Bethany, who of all the anointing narratives is only named in John 12, is a likely candidate to be the original anointing woman in all four texts. The writer of John may have been the last to write the story in his Gospel, but he has the most historical rendition because of claims he has access to an eyewitness (21:24). Possibly earlier witnesses did not associate her name with the event or her identity was purposely disguised.[19]

The most common barrier to this conclusion is that Mary of Bethany, the Johannine actor, is beloved by Jesus and a virtuous Jewish woman. The Lukan woman is described by Simon the Pharisee as a "sinner in the city," so the two could not possibly coincide. I do not find this objection to be insurmountable and it will be further explored. The verb tense used indicates that at the time of this scene, she "used to be" a sinner, but was no longer. In verse 47 the verb translated, "have been forgiven" is a past perfect. Translations have not made this clear, but Jesus sees a woman who has loved much because she has been forgiven much. The frequent misunderstanding that she was a prostitute is unfounded. Barbara Reid gives an extensive list of

15. Bovon *Luke*, 291.

16. Reid, *Choosing*, 109.

17. See Bock *Luke*, 690; Nolland, 352; Hendriksen *Gospel*, 404; Stein *Luke*, 235; Bauckham, *Testimony*, 173; Morris, *Luke*, 425–26.

18. Nolland, 352.

19. Harris, "The Dead Are Restored to Life," 295–326.

the many ways a woman could be considered a "sinner." At that time, a woman who was ill, associated with gentiles, practiced an occupation that was considered unclean, or in any way diverted from the strict limits of behavior determined by the Pharisees, could be considered a sinner known "in the city."[20] Simon Peter—another Simon— calls himself a "sinful man" in 5:7, yet commentators do not speculate that he was immoral in some way. Jesus was also called a "sinner" by the Pharisees when he healed the man born blind on the Sabbath (John 9:16), so this woman was not in bad company. Both Jesus and the anointing woman of Luke 7, whom I propose to be Mary, but not yet from Bethany, were defined as "sinners" by other people."[21]

My solution is that the Lukan narrative took place early in Jesus' ministry close to where Mary was living at that time, in Batanea or in Galilee. She anointed Jesus twice. Her first anointing act was performed once early in Jesus' ministry at her conversion, or shortly after, as recorded in Luke. The important information for the completed portrait of Mary (and Martha) is that she performed a unique event of anointing early in the ministry of Jesus that gained for her legend-like fame with frequent retelling. Then again, she may have already been famous—notoriously. Apparently, she was infamous in a way that was common knowledge in the city. Simon the Pharisee, the host, recognized her and questioned why Jesus did not know of her. What had the tabloids reported about this woman?

A discussion already started above is that behavior, especially by a woman, outside the norms determined by the Pharisees would attract attention and be called sinful. She expressed her sorrow and faith in Jesus by her tears at his feet on this day as recorded by Luke, when she heard he was in the city. Jesus most certainly already knew the woman that came to Simon's house. Now we may surmise that she was Mary. A few years later, she repeated an anointing in Bethany, with a different motivation. Shortly before Passover in thanksgiving for the life of Lazarus and/or in anticipation of Jesus' death she again anointed Jesus. I am not the first, of course, to come up with this observation. Augustine compared the four anointing women, and proposed: "That it was the same Mary who did this deed on two separate occasions, the one being that which Luke has put on record,

20. For the many ways a woman of the first century could be called a sinner see Reid, *Choosing*, 113.

21. Kitzberger, "Transcending," 190.

when she approached him first of all in that remarkable humility, and with those tears, and obtained forgiveness of her sins."[22]

As it was anticipated by Jesus in Mark 14:9: "That wherever the Gospel is preached throughout the world, what she has done will also be told, in memory of her." Much commentary has been expended discussing this issue: if she was to be remembered, why was her name lost?[23] Every Gospel does contain her story, if not her name. I am concluding in this book that her name was not lost. Her name was Mary.

Mary's Two Anointing Acts: It Was Mary All Along.

It was already concluded above that the source of Martha's worries were not her hostess' duties, but Mary's absence; that is, she was not at home to help Martha with her unnamed but overwhelming responsibilities. Perhaps another piece of the new perspective comes into view. Mary had previously pursued some kind of lifestyle that justifiably caused Martha's stress; she is, by all indications, the big sister and their parents are apparently deceased. In Luke 10 Mary is again out of sight, indicated by the imperfect verb meaning habitual activity. In review, I previously concluded that Mary's absence is more similar to abandonment, as indicated by the vocabulary, not just stepping into another room. With this possible history of troublesome behavior, Martha is imploring Jesus to tell Mary to come home to be under her supervision. Do I hear echoes of the Prodigal Son here (Luke 15:11–32)? It never was about Martha needing help with her diaconal duties in the community and Jesus knew it. He understood totally that Martha just wanted Mary within her eyesight. That is why Jesus totally bypasses concern about her overwhelming service, but addresses her worries. As I said at the beginning of this chapter, it is not necessary to insert this hypothesis that builds a background to Mary and Martha's story. Martha wants Mary back, for reason of needing help with responsibilities and no more reason is necessary. But then again, what if . . .?

Now revisit a question I left unanswered earlier, which is the question that originally drove my quest to look carefully at Mary of Bethany. I was puzzled by the unexplained prominence of Mary, not only in popular books of today, but with hints left in the biblical text itself. Why does she have the extra mention in John 11:2? Why is Martha able to leave the house

---

22. Augustine, *Harmony of the Gospels*, chapt 79.

23. Schüssler Fiorenza, *In Memory of Her*, xliii.

to meet Jesus without attracting extra attention, but when Mary leaves the house, a crowd follows her? Why in 11:45 does the narrator mention the many Jews that came to visit Mary, but Martha is omitted? This was my original question: "What is the mystery of Mary?"

If the anointing woman of Luke 7:36–50 is Mary, then she was already known as a "sinner in the city" (7:37). Mary had many resources available to her; she had no apparent financial concerns, she had a special friendship with Jesus, she had siblings, she had access to Jesus' teaching. Apparently— she also had a history. Reasons for Mary's almost, but not quite concealed, prominence raise questions about what information is hidden just beneath the surface. Only a small minority of commentaries notice these subtle hints in the text, and critically move past traditional interpretations.

The first source I read that really set off a spark on the way to uncovering the mystery of Mary of Bethany was Schüssler Fiorenza, who suspects that in an earlier tradition Mary may have had followers around her who were led to believe in Jesus.[24] In a later work of 2002, Yamaguchi is one of the few to notice and agree with this idea[25] that Mary appears as a friend and disciple of Jesus and is also a leader with Judean followers. Prior to the events of John 11 and 12, Mary of Bethany had somehow become well-known and beloved with a devoted following. How could have this happened given that a quick reading of John 11 yields a very unimpressive resume, i.e., she is almost speechless and overcome with grief?

Conway noted that John 11:31 gives the first indication of one of the roles that Mary will play in the narrative: "Unbeknownst to the Jews, she is actually leading them to Jesus."[26] In 11:42, although Mary is not mentioned at this point, Jesus' prayer to the Father mentions: "For the sake of the crowd, so that they may believe that you sent me." This statement makes clear that the presence of the crowd is important to the total scene. Jesus performs the sign, not simply to restore a dead friend to life, but to convince the Jewish onlookers of his identity. Mary was not aware of her importance in bringing a crowd to Jesus, but without her "following" which she led out to meet Jesus, the number of Jewish witnesses, and resultant believers, would not have been so big. She was an attention-getter, and that is what Jesus needed.

---

24. Schüssler Fiorenza, "A Feminist Critical Interpretation," 21–36.

25. Yamaguchi, *Mary & Martha*, 122.

26. Conway, *Men and Women*, 143.

Luke 7:18–35 concerns the ministry of John the Baptist. If there is a connection with the text immediately preceding, Mary may have been a follower of John. She heard Jesus was in her city, found him, and repented of her earlier life with such an extravagant and memorable gesture that this event became legendary. The writer of John finally names her in John 11:2 when Mary is introduced as the one who poured perfume on the Lord and wiped his feet with her hair. Instead of this remark anticipating an event that in John is yet to occur, he is bringing to remembrance Mary's previous anointing with which the Johannine readers are already familiar, either from reading Luke or the oral tradition behind it. I would say that she reprised the act a few years later before Passion Week. To further clarify, I propose that the anointing women in all four Gospels is Mary of Bethany, and she anointed Jesus twice, once early in Jesus' ministry in Galilee when she first repented of her sins, and then a few years later in Bethany when Jesus was on his last journey to Jerusalem.

Famous, or infamous, maybe she was both. Mary attracted attention. If she became a Christ-follower, began a new life-style, and carried out the anointing scene in Luke 7, this conversion added to the attention she attracted. At this point, she could have easily became one of the female followers noted at the beginning of Luke 8. (Remember chapter breaks were inserted later, so the verses at the beginning of chapter 8 may actually continue chapter 7.) In addition, she could also be one of the "seventy" in chapter 10. There appears to be enough precedent for her to be an itinerate follower of Jesus.

Whatever charisma she had as a "sinner in the city," she now turned her gifts into work for Jesus. The old life she led, however well-known it was in the first century, is completely unrecoverable. Now she is remembered for her devotion to Jesus. She served Jesus in his ministry and attracted more believers to Jesus. As she followed Jesus to Jerusalem, she became a leader and teacher herself. Granted Lazarus and/or Martha may have been well-known in their own right, or the family may have been very prominent as discussed in chapter 2—somehow Mary got the attention. Dramatic conversions are memorable and get more attention, even today, more so than the quiet conversions of "background" people like Martha who just "always believed." The reason may now be somewhat less of a mystery, now she is remembered for her devotion to Jesus in whom she found new life. She put her abilities to good use to win followers for Jesus. Meanwhile, Martha has not disappeared; she is influential behind the scenes. Some of us are like that.

10

The New Perspective for an Old Story

NOW WE COME AROUND to the recapitulation of this journey with Mary and Martha. Like so many good things, it started in a conversation with a friend who suggested a devotional that extols the example of Martha over that of Mary needed to be written. We wanted to counter the many popular books that make Mary the prime example to follow, leading to discouragement when so much of our lives appear to be invalidated. My research was undertaken to find the reasons why Martha is so often proclaimed "the lesser" example as compared to her sister Mary. After much preliminary study, the research results morphed into a thesis, and then this book. I certainly experienced some cul-de-sacs! I researched the possibility that Mary was a female Jewish mystic, healer, scholar, political leader, or "saint-like" figure, and always came up empty. Amazingly, the answer to the source of Mary's acclaim was found right in the text itself. She had led a complex life, and that always makes a more interesting story.

Even better than setting one sister above the other was discovering that there are no longer any grounds for not setting both on a pedestal. After looking more carefully at the Gospels, both of the sisters come to life in their own right as the details of their situations emerged. The new perspective offers many reasons for both men and women to aspire to the example of Martha and Mary, who fervently believed and carried out their faith in Jesus in their God-given contrasting ways.

Some things stay the same as in the old interpretations. Martha is still the sister that needs an "attitude adjustment," but it is a much more complex and understandable "correction" than previously imagined. Anyone of us can understand her great concern for her sister, as we care for loved ones—young and old, near and far. Martha still seems to be the stalwart pillar in the home and community, but the challenges of her discipleship are larger than imagined before. The community of Christ does not survive long without her *diakonia*. Mary is still mysterious—she had a past for which she was forgiven and started a new life of evangelism with Jesus. How many of us would like to erase a wayward segment of our lives? She showed the enormity of Jesus' forgiveness in her actions. This may explain why she has received the acclaim all these years, but that does not diminish Martha. A whole new look has emerged for the sisters.

MANY NEW LESSONS: JOHN 11–12

One could say that taken together, the two sisters accomplish what the Samaritan woman (John 4) did alone. Together the sisters are a contrast to the unbelieving Jewish leadership. Separately, Martha elicits self-revelation from Jesus and responds in faith. She represents those early followers of Jesus to the Johannine community just as Peter represented the disciples in Matt. 16:15–19.[1] Mary brings the Jewish people to Jesus, enabling them to witness his power for themselves as the Samaritan woman carried the message to her village. In this way, the narrative purpose for the sisters' separate visits to Jesus becomes clearer. However, they are also working together. Martha is the disciple, who ministered to "insiders," those at home and the people who are already followers of Jesus. "To the Evangelist and his audience, Martha undoubtedly represented the ones who believed before they had seen and understood everything of what Jesus' 'I am' would come to mean."[2] Martha's audience does not need the "signs" noted by John to be necessary for those with marginal belief, i.e., Thomas being an example of needing to "see" (Jn 20:29). She received the "I am" statement from Jesus for her benefit—and the benefit of all of us since who must believe on faith.

Mary, not as a reflection on her own understanding, but on that of the Jews to whom she ministered, led those out to Jesus who needed to see a "sign." In John 11, both sisters approached Jesus with the same remark, "Lord, if you had been here." Any theories as to how this happened that the sisters approached Jesus with the same remark are tentative, but the question is one that all believers ask upon facing a tragedy. "Where were you, Jesus? If you had been here this event would not have occurred." Or, as Martha asked Jesus in Luke 10:40, "Lord, don't you care?" Both sisters approached Jesus with the same remark, and then Jesus gave two different

---

1. Schneiders, *Written*, 106.
2. Ridderbos, *The Gospel*, 400.

responses appropriate for the two different ministries the sisters led. Jesus' response is different for each sister.[3] In his private response to Martha, Jesus focuses on who he is. His public response to Mary is emotional as he matches her weeping. With Martha he talks theology, and with Mary he shares tears. Notably Jesus does not say, "If you believe in the resurrection, why are you wasting your time and your tears?"[4] Jesus does not reprimand anyone for crying. He understands each believer's personality, allows for human sorrow, and it is not a sign of weak faith.

Both Mary and Martha Set the Stage for Jesus

Can we imagine the Gospel of John without the great "I am" statements? Martha set the scene for the last and greatest of them all. "I know that he will arise on the last day," occasioned Jesus' witness about his divinity. If Martha is frequently portrayed as the one who only did practical service and did not take time to study at the feet of Jesus, then where did she learn the theology she demonstrates in this scene with Jesus "on the road?" The answer, as we discovered, is that she was sitting at Jesus' feet along with Mary in the time before the scene in Luke, and no doubt many times later. Her hands may have been busy, but the Spirit spoke while she was actively serving. This great conversation was for those who may have witnessed this interaction, but also for her flock to whom she retold the lesson she heard in her grief, until it was finally written for the untold multitudes whose faith and belief was deepened by her confession.

Martha also sets the stage when she prominently amplifies the magnitude of Jesus' miracle by her words, "He has been dead for four days, he stinks" (11:30). Jesus returned to life a body that had been dead and decomposing. She removes forever any conversation that Lazarus was somehow less than dead. In addition, this miracle was not out of reach of Jesus' divine power, as is the resurrection of all believers since, despite total return to the dust of the earth. In chapter 12, Martha is mentioned one more time where she in some capacity facilitates a dinner in the honor of Jesus. The note that she is again involved with *diakonia* is further evidence that her service was not the original problem to be remedied in the Lukan passage. She is still engaged in her gift and call.

3. Spencer, "You Just Don't," 37–38.

4. Burge, *John*, 331.

Mary's action of falling at his feet and weeping sets the stage for the occasion of Jesus' dramatic and memorable display of emotion. Calvin commented on 11:38: "Christ does not come to the sepulcher as an idle spectator, but like a wrestler preparing for the contest. Therefore no wonder that He groans again, for the violent tyranny of death that he had to overcome stands before His eyes."[5] Jesus desires that as many people as possible will believe and be saved. The emotional scene buys time for more people to come from the house and perhaps the surrounding area to witness the events to come. When Jesus cries, it reinforces his humanity, shows his empathy for the mourners, and/or grief at their unbelief. Mary also elicits an event that gives reason for new insight concerning Jesus. To each sister in turn he shows both his divinity, humanity, and who he really is.

LEADERSHIP IN UNLIKELY PLACES

This new perspective on Mary and Martha teaches us many new lessons that are much richer than the old adage: "Make time for study and don't get overwhelmed with worldly affairs." In particular, new models of leadership come forward that would never be noticed under the old perspective. If one were seeking nominations for leadership positions, the sisters, according to the old portrait, would not likely get the nod. Faced with the death of her brother in John 11, Mary appears to be overcome by catatonic sorrow. Upon approaching Jesus, she falls at his feet and mouths words identical with those her sister had greeted him moments before: "Jesus, if you had been here my brother would not have died" (11:32). Martha appears to take better command of the situation in this scene, i.e., Martha anticipates Jesus' entry into the village and approaches him without waiting to be called. In the face of tragedy, she maintains the necessary composure to engage in a theological discussion that eventually results in Jesus' "I am" statement. Her confession is held up as the equivalent of Peter's confession in the Synoptics and the model Johannine confession according to 20:31. Yet, no one is recorded as witnessing this interchange between Jesus and Martha; no one accompanied her to the edge of the village because she apparently was not the type of person to attract a following. No one told her, "Martha, I will come with you."

Another lesson on leadership comes from Luke 10:38–42, where according to the traditional interpretation, no words come from Mary,

5. Calvin quoted in Ridderbos, *The Gospel*, 402.

apparently setting a positive example by her actions alone. Martha aggressively pursues Jesus for a solution to her sister's absence and asks Jesus to intervene, but she is the one, as the scene is traditionally interpreted, that needs to "calm down." No leader to be found there either. Likewise, Mary is essentially silent in John, only repeating words already spoken, yet Jesus twice commends Mary's behavior (Lk. 10:42; Jn. 12:7). Consistently over the many centuries of Christian interpretation, commentators tended to read examples of "good" and "bad" from both these stories. What kind of example is Jesus extolling for women? Could it be possible that "silent leadership," by actions only, as demonstrated by Mary in both Luke (according to the traditional interpretation) and John, but otherwise without voice or opinion is the illustration of leadership that Jesus recommends for women? Or, if women dare have a theological discussion with a man, it should be done privately? As the new perspective is worked out, one discovers that both Mary and Martha were using their voices to be able to attract the individual followings they had. The Jews from Jerusalem would not have come out to mourn with them if they were silent women.

Leadership can be found in surprising places, in unlikely humans (female), hidden in the shadow of a more momentous event. I pursue the premise that Jesus commissioned both sisters to demonstrate equally valid and essential examples of leadership to make the result of his final sign most effective. The sisters together are ministering to different "flocks" demonstrating "good and good." Together they make access to Jesus' greatest statements of his identity available to the maximum possible number of followers. The previous chapters of this book have stripped away the "sister-versus-sister" preconception from earlier study of both Luke and John, allowing whole new lessons to emerge.

Mary's prior reputation and ability to attract a crowd is an important piece of what Jesus is accomplishing in his final and greatest sign at the end of his public ministry. The climax of narrative tension occurs in 11:42 when Jesus prays out loud: "I knew that you always hear me, but I said this for the benefit of the people standing here, that they may believe that you sent me." Jesus had master-planned the entire Lazarus narrative with the goal of bringing as many people possible out into the open, that they may be brought to belief by the performance of his final sign.

The attraction of many mourners was set into motion at least four days earlier when Jesus waited before arriving in Bethany. Because of Lazarus' death, the Jews from Jerusalem who had come to comfort the sisters had swollen to a crowd. They were already in place in Bethany when Jesus arrived. By not going directly to the house, he was able to call Mary to come to him, and with her came the many Jews consoling her. When he remained outside the house and arranged the ensuing scene to occur outside, Mary was in effect leading the Jews to Jesus, which was more effective than his coming to them. They were then ready to witness Mary's remark, her weeping and kneeling, which in turn released the emotional outburst of Jesus. Finally, they all proceeded to the tomb to witness the greatest and final sign of Jesus.

But what about Martha's entrance, conversation with Jesus, and her confession? Does her role fade in comparison? It is impossible to determine how many people witnessed the conversation between Jesus and Martha. Perhaps disciples were with Jesus, who had traveled with him from the "other side of the Jordan." Someone relayed at least the outline of the conversation including Martha's confession to the writer of John. He could have been a witness himself, or the historic writer interviewed Martha in her later years, which is the likely possibility if only Jesus and Martha are at the scene. First, Martha seems to ask Jesus obliquely for a miracle (11:22), which she believes could be possible if Jesus wills it. In her prior experiences with Jesus, she knows and has witnessed that whatever Jesus asks from the Father, he receives.

Martha's remark, "I know he will rise again in the resurrection at the last day" (11:24), results in Jesus' response, "I am the resurrection and the life." The leadership role of Martha is provoking the revelation that Jesus made about himself which is recorded for all ensuing readers of the Gospel, ancient and modern. Because Martha met Jesus without a large crowd pressing around, this intimate exchange was facilitated. All readers of the passage since have the benefit of this conversation and important disclosure of Jesus' understanding of his impending death. Her leadership qualities, which seem to have missed obvious notice in the first centuries, are also being missed in the twenty-first as well. But Jesus gifted her and encouraged her call.

Still another important observation is that Jesus' interaction with Martha precedes the actual carrying out of the sign. Normally Jesus first performs the miracle, and then provides the explanation. Therefore, Martha's confession concerning Jesus as the Christ is absolutely not a result of witnessing the raising of Lazarus. Her confession is purely the response to

Jesus revealing himself verbally as the "resurrection and the life."[6] Likewise, Mary also confesses and worships Jesus physically by her actions. Neither Martha nor Mary needs a visible sign to facilitate belief.

Whether Jesus intended likewise to continue a discussion with Mary is unknown. Perhaps it was not possible because of the crowd that followed her. Perhaps he was hoping for a verbal confession from Mary in front of the crowd, which did not happen. Perhaps it happened just the way Jesus intended. What they did see was her worship and adoration at his feet. The narrator records both sisters greeting Jesus with the same words, "Lord, if you had been here my brother would not have died." Jesus' different response to the identical statements makes possible a parallel comparison between Jesus' contrasting modes of consoling the mourners. In addition, imagine Jesus sighing, *Do they really think I could not have healed Lazarus from a distance if that was my plan; I have done it before!* e.g., the official's son of John 4:43–54. Jesus is already teaching them that in the future he will not always be physically with them, but present in Spirit.

Mary of Bethany's most important leadership function is leading the Jews of Jerusalem. One may ask how this is possible, considering at first glance that Mary does not appear in the text in any obvious leadership roles. She is certainly not very vocal and when she does speak once, it is not her own spontaneous speech. Looking closer, I conclude that Mary is the reason for the Jews coming out to Bethany to meet Jesus and to witness the subsequent miracle. In 11:42, although Mary is not mentioned at this point, Jesus' prayer spoken aloud to the Father proclaims, "For the sake of the crowd, so that they may believe that you sent me." This statement makes clear that the presence of the crowd is important to the total scene. Jesus performs the sign, not only to restore a dead friend to life, but also to convince the Jewish onlookers of his identity. Mary was probably not aware of her importance in bringing a crowd to Jesus, but without her "followers" which she led out to meet Jesus, the number of Jewish witnesses and resultant believers, would not have been so large.

The narrative purpose for the sisters' separate visits to Jesus becomes clear. Jesus gave two different responses appropriate for the two different ministries the sisters led.[7] They are working together. Martha is Jesus' disciple, drawing on the portrayal from Luke, who ministered to "insiders," those who visited her home, in the village, and among those who are already

---

6. Schneiders, *Written That You May Believe*, 106.

7. Kitzberger, "Mary of Bethany and Mary of Magdala," 578.

followers of Jesus. "To the Evangelist and his audience, Martha undoubtedly represented those who believed before they had seen everything of what Jesus' 'I am' would come to mean."[8] Martha's audience consists of those who did not need the "signs" noted by John to be necessary for those with marginal belief, such as Thomas being an example of needing to "see" (20:29). Martha elicits self-revelation from Jesus and responds verbally in faith. She receives the "I am" statement from Jesus not only for her benefit, but also for the benefit of all readers since. Since the time that Jesus left earth, every believer since is one who must believe without seeing: "Blessed are those who have not seen and yet have believed" (20:29).

Mary brings the Jews of Jerusalem to Jesus, enabling them to witness his power and demonstration of his identity for themselves. Mary, not as a reflection on her own understanding, but on that of the Jews to whom she ministers, led those out to Jesus who needed to see a "sign." Mary by her example and actions shows who Jesus is and how he is to be worshipped. In a surprising number of ways, both Mary and Martha exercise exemplary leadership, to be imitated by both men and women.

Both Mary and Martha Set Precedence for Footwashing at Dining Event

In her anointing of his feet, Mary first sets the footwashing example(s) before Jesus, who then demonstrates the same servant-leadership at the following dinner of John 13.[9] In a way, she may have led Jesus himself, by setting this example, which he followed a few days later. This act of serving was another example of Mary's leadership. It was established in chapter 9 above that Mary was the probable original actor from which all the anointing stories were modeled. As Jesus predicted in Mark 14:9: "Wherever the Gospel is told, what she has done will be remembered." As the story was retold and rewritten in the other Gospels, she was indeed remembered. Jesus himself remembered her remarkable show of devotion as a servant when he in turn washed the feet of those "he loved until the end" (13:1).

By intruding on the dining scene and anointing Jesus' feet, Mary served to bring out the true character of Judas. Mary's act provides Jesus with the opportunity to reveal the truth about his imminent death.[10] Be-

8. Ridderbos, *The Gospel*, 400.

9. Kitzberger, "Transcending" 191.

10. Beirne, *Women and Men*, 153.

fore this occasion, he made veiled references to being 'lifted up' (Jn 3:14; 8:21–22, 28a; 12:32) which are finally explained by the narrator's comment in 12:33. Mary anticipated the day of his burial and gave Jesus the stage on which to explain it before Judas entered the scene.

Martha in turn provided the backdrop for Mary's act of anointing. Without someone to design the venue, whether it was in providing the house, arranging the food, sending out the invitations, or officiating as "mistress of ceremonies," Martha made this unique worship event possible. Jesus enjoyed an evening with friends before he was "lifted up." The people who make these events happen are exercising their gifts and discipleship. They worship by making worship possible. This contribution was meant to be noticed as her *diakonos* was mentioned in John 12:2. Within the same chapter, Jesus himself mentions serving: "My Father will honor the one who *diakonos* me" (12:26).[11] It appears that "service" is no meager form of discipleship and Martha was indeed serving Jesus. Then Jesus repeated a dinner a few days later, where I see Mary, Martha, and Lazarus attending. Mary and Martha foreshadow Jesus' acts as a servant leader, which he demonstrates at the event of John 13, by washing feet and serving at the table.

MANY NEW LESSONS: LUKE 10:38–42

I set out on this thesis journey to free women, and men, from the tyranny of trying to prioritize the activity of Mary, when Martha's duties take up all their time. Amazingly, my research found this is far from the lesson of the story. Women are empowered by these pericopes to a far greater extent than I ever imagined. In both Gospels, the fact that the main characters are women does not even come into consideration. Mary and Martha go far beyond teaching women to choose their priorities wisely. They teach all men and women to have faith as they struggle with decisions concerning their ministry and discipleship. Mary must go against Martha's wishes that she stay home, Martha must struggle with letting her leave and continuing to carry on the ministries in her community alone. In John, they are different leaders of two groups of believers in different stages of their understanding, as they struggle to understand their own grief and persevere in their faith in face of temptation.

As a result of my research I believe the characters are much richer, with many more possibilities for interpretation. The Lukan narrative teaches far

11. O'Day and Hylen, *John*, 121.

more than, "women are allowed to learn," and "take time for quiet study." The Johannine narrative shows Mary and Martha, who incidentally are women, as major players with Jesus in teaching the truth about himself, the truth about his resurrection, and the resurrection of all believers. Many new possibilities for preaching and teaching have opened as a result of this new perspective.

11

Many New Perspectives for Mary and Martha

NEW APPLICATIONS FROM A NEW PERSPECTIVE

How MANY CHRISTIANS, PAST and present, when experiencing a tragedy have cried, "Jesus, where were you? You were not here when I needed you. If you had been here, you could have prevented this." The fact that both sisters are recorded as greeting Jesus with the same refrain may indicate that the author intends to illustrate two individual and uniquely appropriate responses to a tragedy. Martha and Mary asked exactly the same thing, and they invoked two different responses from Jesus.[1] In his private response to Martha, Jesus reveals his power and position. His public response to Mary is emotional as he matches her weeping. With Martha he explains himself, and with Mary he shares tears.

Notably Jesus does not say, "If you believe in the resurrection, why are you wasting your time and your tears?"[2] Showing emotions or questioning is not a sign of weak faith. Jesus affirms in the following chapters that he is always with his disciples, and they should trust him in his absence as when he is physically present.[3] "Abiding" is a Johannine motif. Jesus will be near and comfort even after the ascension as he prepares his disciples for his

---

1. Spencer, "You Just Don't Understand," 37–38.
2. Burge, *John*, 323.
3. Schneiders, "Death in a Community," 51.

absence in the following chapters of the Gospel. In this passage, he shows Mary and Martha that he was with them through the whole incident, and will be in the future.

The writer of John is presenting both Mary and Martha as female disciples of Jesus who learned from him as students would learn from a rabbi, when Martha refers to him as the "Teacher" (11:28). Not only were they learning from him, but putting their knowledge to use by actively leading ministries of their own. Both women are portrayed in leadership roles. Martha represents those early followers of Jesus to the Johannine community just as Peter represented the disciples in Matthew 16:15–19.[4] Mary is shown as leading the Jews of Jerusalem out to Jesus (11:31) visibly demonstrating proper devotion and pointing them to the source of their salvation (12:3). In the next chapter, Jesus emphatically defends her role to Judas, "Let her alone" (12:7). By extension, this is the message to everyone who would restrict the ministry and calls of women anywhere.

In John, Mary and Martha are different leaders of two groups of believers in different stages of understanding, even as they are struggling to understand their own grief. Women in leadership positions must meet those Christians to whom they are preaching and teaching where they are in their journey. Some believers need an object lesson and actual demonstration of how to worship and serve. Other Christians need a theology lesson, which Martha received and passed on to her circle of influence as well as future generations. Different leaders may have a more appropriate style for each group, and those who are leaders should strive to know who they are and when to apply which leadership approach. Both Mary and Martha recognized who they were as disciples called by Jesus, and even in their personal grief both reinforced and shepherded their following as appropriate.

Models of leadership have too often conformed to worldly standards of what a leader should look like. The result has been much grief and disappointment, not to mention the loss of so much leadership talent to the church. The servant model of leadership after Jesus' example has not been the preferred model, because these are exactly the people who by human appearances are frequently overlooked when choosing leaders (cf, Lk. 22:24–27).

Until very recently, the rare occasions when women have had the opportunity to lead, they had to conform to the masculine paradigm of male

4. Schneiders, *Written*, 106.

leadership such as have a commanding loud voice, big stature, and other traits that are generally regarded as "masculine." However, these qualities describe leadership from the human perspective. How many good leaders have been lost to the church because certain persons just did not "look" or "act" the part, as humans have determined that leadership should appear? Many "Marys" and "Marthas" have been passed over as not having leadership potential just as their actual functions in John 11 have been diminished until invisible. We must look at potential leaders with the eyes of Jesus and not of men.

Perhaps the most important application is comfort to those left behind when loved ones leave family to pursue ministry at a distance. The sisters speak out of a deep yearning for presence, intimacy, and community in John, "Lord, if you had been here, our brother would still be here, and we would be together."[5] This seems to parallel a theme from Luke 10:38–42 where Martha's chief concern, according to this thesis, is that Mary "has left her alone." In both Luke and John, Martha longs to have her family complete, near her, in her care.

Many parents have difficulty with their children who decide to go into foreign missions in far reaches of the world. Jesus encouraged Martha by telling her that Mary's choice was good. So far, the most rewarding response I have had to this thesis occurred when explaining it on two different occasions to two different pastors. They both immediately related the conflict of a relative's family or a parishioner's family, who could not understand a son or daughter's desire to leave home, and serve in the mission field far from home. It also never occurred to me that this application was also meaningful to a family with a son in the military who related to me a similar response. They were not happy about their son being far away and in possible danger, but serving his country was his call and career. They heard from Jesus that it was a good call and it would not be taken away from him. To families in this situation, the application speaks strongly, and who would have thought this could be found in the Mary and Martha story?

At the same time, not all Christians are called to go great distances. The families who remain at home have ministries nurturing believers who live in their neighborhood. Martha was not confined to the kitchen and house. Beyond the unnamed village where this pericope is located, there were the ill and needy in the neighborhood and community, the children and families that needed education. New converts needed to be instructed

5. Schneiders, "Death," 48.

and discipled. This is an equal and valid calling. Believers should not allow themselves to be caught up in worry and carry the burdens alone. In the following narrative of Luke 11:1–4, Jesus teaches his disciples to pray. Whether Luke intended a connection or not, it follows nicely that the antidote for worry is prayer. Jesus cares and knows our needs better than we know them ourselves. Martha approached him with what she thought was her biggest concern, but Jesus recognized the deeper need.

Jesus is with our loved ones when they are away doing his work. Or, if you are the one far from home, Jesus watches your "village" in your absence. Certainly women learn at the feet of Jesus, as men do. Certainly it is important to spend time at the feet of Jesus. Beyond this point, Mary and Martha illustrate that already early in his ministry, women rose from their knees and followed Jesus out to minister among strangers, alongside the male disciples (Lk 8:1–3).

It is a grave injustice to the characters, and greatly misinforms the teachings of both Luke 10:38–42 and John 11–12, to approach the passage with a view that one sister has the "correct" approach to Jesus and the other the "wrong." If Martha has a weakness, it is that she likes to have her friends and family nearby. In Luke her main complaint is, "Don't you care that my sister has left me alone?" In John it is, "If you had been here, Lazarus would be alive, and we would all be together."[6] Who can't identify with that? No one can fault her for wanting friends and family together! It must have been a bittersweet joy for her, as John records in the next chapter, to have friends and all her siblings together, and be "serving" once again. Yet, she must have suspected the scene would never repeat itself.

With this new interpretation of Mary and Martha drawing from John 11 (and Luke 10), the old question, "Are you a Mary or a Martha?" can be thankfully put to rest. It is not a question anymore of whether a woman is more interested in housework than study, or the active life rather than the contemplative, or some other such "appropriate to women" application. Now "Are you a Martha or a Mary?" refers to the kind of ministry in which she is engaged and the demands of her call. All the "Marthas" are to be encouraged as pastors as Martha was serving the insiders, those who were already believers. "Marys" are laboring as evangelists to the "skeptics who must see to believe," and more accurately stated, women and men must be supported to practice their ministries in the many ways appropriate to the believers they are serving.

6. Spencer, "You Just Don't Understand," 37.

NEW LIFE FOR MARY AND MARTHA

Martha and Mary seemed to be crotchety old aunts when I began my research. They were not very likeable, very tiring, and certainly did not have any new stories to tell. Everything they could say had been said many times in countless books, devotions, and sermons. The result was always the same: the listener was pulled to conform to one example, but reality pulled into the other direction. One left their house with the taste of stale cookies and weak coffee. This journey with Mary and Martha started when a pastor friend suggested that a devotional that extols the example of Martha over that of Mary needed to be written to counterweigh the popular books written about Mary. Without her prodding, research on this topic would not have seemed worth pulling a few commentaries off the shelf. I offer thanks to her for the push in the direction of Mary and Martha. After I got started, I could not let go of the conundrum, and with such an investment in research already completed, it was an easy decision to continue working with the ladies. In the meantime, a whole new opinion of the old aunts opened up.

I started research with the aim to get to the truth of Mary and Martha. The route to a new perspective turned out to be more circuitous, but also more rewarding than I expected. I always was a "Mary" and I do not mean only in the name I inherited from a grandmother! As a youngster, I liked to study the Bible stories, but as a young woman, I was discouraged from serious study of theology at the college level and beyond. After marriage and children, I led what was traditionally called a "Martha" life for several decades. I made some career changes and earned college degrees, before I found my call in seminary study. After the years of raising my kids, moving with my husband because of his Army career, getting settled and then packing up again, the time was right for me to pursue a long-time interest and I started studying biblical Greek. Earlier, I would have said that my "study time" and my "service time," instead of being integrated within the days, stretched into years when I did one or the other almost exclusively for uninterrupted periods. Now I realize I was building both constantly—all the time. My walk with Jesus was not lessor when I was rocking a baby and my Bible gathered dust at my bedside table. Both activities are worship, both discipleships are needed. All service in Jesus' name is study; all study is service.

Now the most amazing realization is how firmly the familiar interpretation is entrenched in the minds of those who have heard the story for years. I am very aware that this new look at the narrative threatens to upset about 1800 years of received interpretation. There is a lot of resistance to considering a new view of the sisters. I suspect that I will continue for the rest of my lifetime to read constantly, "Jesus was revolutionary for his time. He empowered women to leave housework and encouraged them to learn at his feet." Yes, I agree with that and I am thankful for these words. But, I will scream at the page: "There is so much more to Mary and Martha!" Martha and Mary influenced their followers near and far; they furthered the teaching of Jesus and increased the number of Christ-believers with their understanding gained at the feet of Jesus.

Over the years, the story has nurtured Christians, certainly women, and men as well. It gave women permission to study and take time from their endless work. If Luke 10:38–42 accomplishes this much comfort, assurance, and empowerment for women, that is the strength of the scriptures. They are durable, and truth manages to come though even with less than ideal handling by the "historic readers." Regardless of how my interpretation stands up to critical review, the alternative view presented in this new perspective yields a rich harvest of new insights for diverse discipleship.

Bibliography

Alexander, Loveday C. "Sisters in Adversity: Retelling Martha's Story." In *A Feminist Companion to Luke*, edited by Amy-Jill Levine, 197–213. Cleveland: The Pilgrim Press, 2004.

Arlandson, James Malcolm. *Women, Class, and Society in Early Christianity: Models From Luke-Acts.* Peabody: Hendrickson, 1997.

Balch, David L. and Carolyn Osiek. *Early Christian Families in Context: An Interdisciplinary Dialogue.* Grand Rapids: Eerdmans, 2003.

Baltz, Frederick W. *Lazarus and the Fourth Gospel Community.* Lewiston: The Edwin Mellen Press, 1996.

Bauckham, Richard. *Gospel Women.* Grand Rapids: Eerdmans, 2002.

———. *The Testimony of the Beloved Disciple.* Grand Rapids: Baker, 2007.

Bauer, E., W.F. Arndt, F.W. Gingrich and W.D. Danker, eds. *A Greek-English Lexicon of the New Testament and Other Early Christian Literature,* 3rd ed. Chicago: The University of Chicago Press, 2001.

Beasley-Murray, George R. *John,* WBC. Nashville: Nelson Reference & Electronic, 1999.

Beirne, Margaret M. *Women and Men in the Fourth Gospel.* New York: Sheffield Academic Press, 2003.

Blomberg, Craig L. *Contagious Holiness: Jesus' Meals with Sinners.* Downers Grove: InterVarsity, 2005.

———. *The Historical Reliability of John's Gospel: Issues & Commentary.* Downers Grove: InterVarsity Press, 2001.

———. *Jesus and the Gospels: An Introduction and Survey.* 2nd ed. Nashville: B&H Publishing Group, 2009.

Bock, Darrell L. *Luke* 9:51–24:53, BECNT. Grand Rapids: Baker, 1994.

Bovon, François. *A Commentary on the Gospel of Luke* 1:1—9:50. Minneapolis: Fortress Press, 2002.

Brant, Jo-Anne A. *Dialogue and Drama: Elements of Greek Tragedy in the Fourth Gospel.* Peabody: Hendrickson, 2004.

———. *John.* Grand Rapids: Baker, 2011.

Brauch, Manfred T. *Abusing Scripture: The Consequences of Misreading the Bible.* Downers Grove: IVP Academic, 2009.

Brown, Raymond E. *The Community of the Beloved Disciple.* New York: Paulist Press, 1979.

Brutscheck, Jutta. *Die Maria-Marta-Erzählung: Eine redaktionskritishe Untersuchung zu Lk* 10,38–42. Frankfurt am Main: Peter Hanstein Verlag, 1986.

Bucknall, Alison M. "Martha's Work and Mary's Contemplation: The Women of the Mildmay Conference and the Keswisk Convention, 1856–1900." In *Gender and Christian Religion,* edited by R.N. Swanson, 405–420. Woodbridge, Eng: Boydell Press, 1998.

Burge, Gary M. *John,* NIVAC. Grand Rapids: Zondervan, 2000.

Caird, G. B. *The Gospel of St. Luke.* Baltimore: Penguin, 1963.

Capper, Brian J. "Two Types of Discipleship in Early Christianity." *JTS* 52 (2001): 105–23.

Carroll, John T. *Luke: A Commentary.* Louisville: Westminster John Knox Press, 2012.

Carson, D. A. *The Gospel According to John.* Grand Rapids: Eerdmans, 1991.

Carter, Warren. "Getting Martha out of the Kitchen: Luke 10:38–42 Again." In *A Feminist Companion to Luke,* edited by Amy-Jill Levine, 214–231. Cleveland: The Pilgrim Press, 2001.

Charlesworth, James H. *Jesus and Archaeology.* Grand Rapids: Eerdmans, 2006.

Christ-Von Wedel, Christine. "*Die Perikope von Martha and Maria bei Erasmus und den Reformatoren.*" *Zwingliana* 27 (2000): 103–115.

Chung, Sook Ja. "Bible Study: Women's Ways of Doing Mission in the Story of Mary and Martha." *International Review of Mission* 93 (2004): 9–16.

Coakley, J. F. "The Anointing at Bethany and the Priority of John." *JBL* 107 (1988): 241–256.

Coffey, Kathy. *Hidden Women of the Gospels.* New York: Crossroad, 1997.

Cohick, Lynn H. *Women in the World of the Earliest Christians: Illuminating Ancient Ways of Life.* Grand Rapids: Baker Academic, 2009.

Collins, John N. *Diakonia: Re-interpreting the Ancient Sources.* New York: Oxford University Press, 1990.

_____. "Did Luke Intend a Disservice to Women in the Martha and Mary Story?" *Biblical Theology Bulletin* 28 (1998): 104–111.

Constable, Giles. *Three Studies in Medieval Religious and Social Thought.*Cambridge: Cambridge Uiversity Press, 1998.

Conway, Colleen M. *Men and Women in the Fourth Gospel: Gender and Johannine Characterization.* Atlanta: Society of Biblical Literature, 1999.

_____. "*Speaking Through Ambiguaity: Minor Characters in the Fourth Gospel.*" *Biblical Interpretation* 10 (2002): 324–341.

Corley, Kathleen E. *Private Women, Public Meals.* Peabody: Hendrickson, 1993.

Craddock, Fred B. *Luke: Interpretation.* Louisville: John Knox Press, 1990.

Culpepper, R. Alan. *Anatomy of the Fourth Gospel: A Study in Literary Design.* Philadelphia: Fortress Press, 1983.

_____."The Johannine *Hypodeigma*: A Reading of John 13." *Semeia* 53 (1991): 133–149.

D'Angelo, Mary Rose. "Women in Luke-Acts: A Redactional View." *JBL* 109 (1990): 441–461.

Davies, Margaret. *Rhetoric and Reference in the Fourth Gospel.* New York: Sheffield Press, 1992.

Davies, Stevan. "Women in the Third Gospel and the New Testament Apocrypha." In *Women Like This: New Perspectives on Jewish Women in the Greco-Roman World,*edited by Amy-Jill Levine, 185–197. Atlanta: Scholars Press, 1991.

DeConick, April D. *Voices of the Mystics: Early Christian Discourse in the Gospels of John and Thomas and Other Ancient Christian Literature.* Sheffield: Sheffield Academic Press, 2001.

Dodd, C. H. *Historical Tradition in the Fourth Gospel.* Cambridge: University Press, 1963.

Duke, Paul D. *Irony in the Fourth Gospel.* Atlanta: John Knox Press, 1985.

Dunderberg, Ismo. "Vermittlung statt karitativer Tätigkeit? Überlegungen zu John N. Collins' Interpretation von Diakonia," in *Diakonische Konturen: Theologie im Kontext sozialer Arbeit,* ed., Volker Herrmann, Rainer Merz, Heinz Schmidt 171–183. Heidelberg: Universitätsverlag, 2003.

Esler, Philip F, and Ronald A. Piper. *Lazarus, Mary and Martha: Social-Scientific Approaches to the Gospel of John.* Minneapolis: Fortress Press, 2006.

Estes, Douglas. *The Questions of Jesus in John: Logic, Rhetoric and Persuasive Discourse.* Bosten: Brill, 2013.

Fee, Gordon D. "One Thing is Needful? Luke 10:42." In *Essays in Honour of Bruce M. Metzger,* edited by E. J. Epp and G. D. Fee, 61–75. Oxford: Clarendon Press, 1981.

Fee, Gordon D. and Douglas Stuart. *How to Read the Bible for All Its Worth.* 2nd ed. Grand Rapids: Zondervan, 1981.

Fehribach, Adeline. *The Women in the Life of the Bridegroom.* Collegeville, Minn: The Liturgical Press, 1998.

Fitzmyer, Joseph A. *The Gospel According to Luke X–XXIV.* New York: Doubleday, 1981.

Garland, David E. *Luke,* ECNT. Grand Rapids: Zondervan, 2011.

Getty-Sullivan, Mary Ann. *Women in the New Testament.* Collegeville: The Liturgical Press, 2001.

Gonzales, Justo L. *Luke.* Louisville: Westminster John Knox Press, 2010.

Green, Joel B. *The Gospel of Luke,* NICNT. Grand Rapids: Eerdmans, 1997.

Grumett, David. "Action and/or Contemplation? Allegory and liturgy in the reception of Luke 10:338-42." *Scottish Journal of Theology* 2 (2006): 125–139.

Häfner, Gerd. "Die Salbung Jesu durch Maria (John 12:1-8): Zwei Rätsel and drei Lösungen." *Biblische Notizen* 122 (2004): 81–104.

Harris, Murray, J. "The Dead Are Restored to Life: Miracles of Revivification in the Gospels." In *The Miracles of Jesus,* edited by David Wenham and Craig Blomberg. Sheffield: JSOT Press, 1986.

Hearon, Holly E. "Luke 10:38-42." *Interpretation* 58 (2004): 393–395.

Hendriksen, William. *Luke,* NTC. Grand Rapids: Baker, 1997.

Hentschel, Anni. *Diakonia im Neuen Testament: Studien zur Semantik unter besonderer Berücksichtigung der Rolle von Frauen.* Tübingen: Morhr Siebeck, 2007.

Howard, James M. "The Significance of Minor Characters in the Gospel of John." *Bibliotheca Sacra* 163 (2006): 63–78.

Hutson, Christopher Roy. "Martha's Choice: A Pastorally Sensitive Reading of Luke 10:38-42." *Restoration Quarterly* 45 (2003): 139–150.

Jeffrey, David Lyle. *Luke.* Grand Rapids: Brazos Press, 2012.

Johnson, L.T. *Luke,* SPS. Collegeville: The Liturgical Press, 1991.

Keener, Craig S. *The Gospel of John: A Commentary,* Vol. 2 . Peabody: Hendrickson, 2003.

_____.*Paul, Women and Wives: Marriage and Women's Ministry in the Letters of Paul.* Peabody: Hendrickson, 1992.

Kilgallen, John J. "A Suggestion Regarding *gar* in Luke 10:42." *Biblica* 73 (1992): 255–258.

_____. "Martha and Mary: Why at Luke 10:38-42?" *Biblica* 84 (2003): 554–561.

King, Rosemary. "Martha and Mary." *The Expository Times* 121 (2010):459–461.

Kim, Jean K. *Woman and Nation: An Intercontextual Reading of the Gospel of John from a Postcolonial Feminist Perspective.* Boston: Brill Academic Publishers, Inc., 2004.

Kitzberger, Ingrid Rosa. "Mary of Bethany and Mary of Magdala: Two Female Characters in the Johannine Passion Narrative." *NTS* 41(1995): 564–586.

_____."Transcending Gender Boundaries." In *A Feminist Companion to John.* Vol. 1. edited by Amy-Jill Levine, 173–207. Cleveland: The Pilgrim Press, 2003.

Klein, William W., Craig L. Blomberg, and Robert L. Hubbard Jr. *Introduction to Biblical Interpretation.* 2nd. Ed. Nashville: Thomas Nelson, 2004.

Koester, Craig R. *Symbolism in the Fourth Gospel: Meaning, Mystery, Community.* Minneapolis: Fortress Press, 2003.

Kohlenberger, John R. III, Edward W. Goodrick and James A. Swanson, *The Greek English Concordance to the New Testament.* Grand Rapids: Zondervan, 1997.

Koperski, Veronica. "Women and Discipleship in Luke 10:38–42 and Acts 6:1–7: the Literary Context of Luke-Acts." In *A Feminist Companion to Luke,* edited by Amy-Jill Levine, 161–196. Cleveland: The Pilgrim Press, 2004.

Köstenberger, Andreas J. *John,* BECNT. Grand Rapids: Baker Academic, 2004.

Lee, Dorothy. *Flesh and Glory.* New York: Crossroad, 2002.

_____.*Hallowed in Truth and Love: Spirituality in the Johannine Literature.* Eugene: Wipf and Stock, 2012.

_____." Martha and Mary: Levels of Characterization in Luke and John." In *Characters and Characterization in the Gospel of John,* edited by Christopher W. Skinner, 197–220. New York: Bloomsbury, 2013.

Levine, Amy-Jill. *A Feminist Companion to Luke.* Cleveland: The Pilgrim Press, 2001.

_____.*The Misunderstood Jew: The Church and the Scandal of the Jewish Jesus.* San Francisco: HarperCollins, 2006.

Luter, Boyd and Kathy McReynolds. *Women as Christ's Disciples.* Grand Rapids: Baker Books, 1997.

Maccini, Robert Gordon. *Her Testimony is True: Women as Witnesses According to John.* Sheffield: Sheffield Academic Press Ltd, 1996.

Magness, Jody. *Stone and Dung, Oil and Spit: Jewish Daily Life in the Time of Jesus.* Grand Rapids: Eerdmans, 2011.

Maline, Bruce J. *The New Testament World: Insights from Cultural Anthropology.* Louisville: John Knox Press, 2001.

Malone, Mary T. *Women & Christianity: The First Thousand Years.* Maryknoll: Orbis, 2001.

Marshall, I. Howard. *The Gospel of Luke,* NIGTC. Grand Rapids: Michigan, 1978.

McKnight, Scott. "Source Criticism." In *Interpreting the N.T: Essays on Methods and Issues,* edited by David Alan Black and David S. Dockery, 74–105. Nashville: Broadman and Holman, 2001.

Meyers, Eric M. "The Problems of Gendered Space in Syro-Palestinian Domestic Architecture: The Case of Roman-Period Galilee." In *Early Christian Families in Context: An Interdisciplinary Dialogue,* edited by David L. Balch and Carolyn Osiek, 44–72. Grand Rapids: Eerdmans, 2003.

Michaels, J. Ramsey. *John,* NIBC. Peabody: Hendrickson, 1989.

Moloney, Francis J. "Can Everyone be Wrong? A Reading of John 11:1–12:8." *New Testament Studies* 49 (2003): 505–527.

_____. "The Faith of Martha and Mary: A Narrative Approach to John 11:17–40." *Biblica* 75 (1994): 471–493.

Moltmann-Wendel, Elizabeth. *The Women Around Jesus.* New York: Crossroad, 1992.

Morris, Leon. *Expository Reflections on the Gospel of John.* Grand Rapids: Baker Book House, 1988.

Mullins, Michael. *The Gospel of John.* Dublin: The Columba Press, 2003.

Neyrey, Jerome H. *The Gospel of John in Cultural and Rhetorical Perspective.* Grand Rapids: Eerdmans, 2009.

_____."What's Wrong with this Picture? John 4, Cultural Stereotypes of Women, and Public and Private Space." In *A Feminist Companion to John*, edited by Amy-Jill Levine, 98–125. Cleveland: The Pilgrim Press, 2001.

Nolland, John. *Luke 9:21–18:34*, WBC. Dallas: Word Books, 1999.

North, Wendy Sproston. "Jesus' Prayer in John 11." In *Old Testament in the New Testament*, edited by Steve Moyise, 164–180. Sheffield: Sheffield Academic Press, 2000.

Ockinga, Boyo. "The Tradition History of the Mary-Martha Pericope in Luke 10:38–42." In *Ancient History in a Modern University*, Vol. 2, edited by T.W. Hillard and Rosalinde Anne Kearsley, 93–97. Grand Rapids: Eerdmans, 1998.

Osborn, Grant R. "Redaction Criticism." In *Interpreting the New Testament: Essays on Methods and Issues*, edited by David Alan Black and David S. Dockery, 128–149. Nashville: Broadman & Holman, 2001.

O' Day, Gail R. and Susan E. Hylen. *John*, WBC. Louisville: Westminster John Knox Press, 2006.

O' Grady, John. *According to John: The Witness of the Beloved Disciple*. New York: Paulist Press, 1999.

Osiek, Carolyn and Margaret Y. MacDonald. *A Woman's Place: House Churches in Earliest Christianity*. Minneapolis: Augsburg Press, 2006.

Peters, Diane E. "The Life of Martha of Bethany by Pseudo-Marcilia." *Theological Studies* 58 (1997): 441–460.

_____. *The Many Faces of Martha of Bethany*. Ottawa: Novalis, 2008.

Pink, Arthur W. *Exposition of the Gospel of John*. Grand Rapids: Zondervan, 1968.

Pixner, Bargil. *With Jesus through Galilee According to the Fifth Gospel*. Rosh Pina: Corazin Publishing, 1992.

Powell, Mark Allan. "Narrative Criticism." In *Hearing the New Testament: Strategies for Interpretation*, edited by Joel B. Green, 239–253. Grand Rapids: Eerdmans, 1995.

Powell, Mark Allan. *What Is Narrative Criticism?* Minneapolis: Fortress Press, 1990.

Rebera, Ranjini. "Polarity or Partnership? Retelling the Story of Martha and Mary from Asian Women's Perspective." *Semeia* 78 (1997): 93–107.

Reese, Jeanene P. "Co-Workers in the Lord: A Biblical Theology of Partnership." *Restoration Quarterly* 45 (2003): 106–114.

Reid, Barbara E. *Women in the Gospel of Luke: Choosing the Better Part?* Collegeville: The Liturgical Press, 1996.

Riesner, Rainer. "Bethany Beyond the Jordan (John 1:28) Topography, Theology and History in the Fourth Gospel." *Tyndale Bulletin* 38 (1987): 29–63.

Resseguie, James L. *Narrative Criticism of the New Testament: An Introduction*. Grand Rapids: Baker Academic, 2005.

_____. *Spiritual Landscape: Images of the Spiritual Life in the Gospel of Luke*. Peabody: Hendrickson, 2004.

_____.*The Strange Gospel*. Leiden: Brill, 2001.

Ridderbos, Herman N. *The Gospel According to John*. Grand Rapids: Eerdmans, 1997.

Ringe, Sharon H. *Luke*. Louisville: Westminster John Knox Press, 1995.

Ryle, J.C. *Luke*, Crossway Classic Commentaries. Wheaton: Crossway, 1997.

Sanders, E. P. *Paul and Palestinian Judaism*. Minneapolis: Fortress, 1977.

Sanford, John A. *Mystical Christianity: A Psychological Commentary on the Gospel of John*. New York: Crossroad, 2000.

Schneiders, Sandra M. "Death in the Community of Eternal Life: History, Theology, and Spirituality in John 11." *Interpretation* 41 (1987): 44–56.

_____. "Women in the Fourth Gospel and the Role of Women in the Contemporary Church." *Biblical Theology Bulletin* 12 (1982): 35–45.

_____.*Written That You May Believe: Encountering Jesus in the Fourth Gospel*. New York: Crossroad, 1999.

Schüssler Fiorenza, Elisabeth. *But She Said: Feminist Practices of Biblical Interpretation*. Beacon Press: Boston, 1992.

_____. "A Feminist Critical Interpretation for Liberation: Martha and Mary: Lk. 10:38–42." *Religion and Intellectual Life* 3 (1986): 21–36.

_____. *In Memory of Her*. New York: Crossroad, 1983.

Seim, Turid Karlsen. *The Double Message: Patterns of Gender in Luke-Acts*. New York: T&T Clark International, 1990.

Smith, D. Moody. *John,* ANTC. Nashville: Abingdon, 1999.

Smith, Dennis E. *From Symposium to Eucharist: The Banquet in the Early Christian World*. Minneapolis: Fortress Press, 2003.

Spencer, Aida Besancon. "Jesus' Treatment of Women in the Gospels." In *Discovering Biblical Equality: Complementarity Without Heirarchy*, edited by Ronald W. Pierce and Rebecca Merrill Groothuis, 126–141. Downers Grove: InterVarsity Press, 2004.

Spencer, F. Scott. *Salty Wives, Spirited Mothers, and Savvy Widows: Capable Women of Purpose and Persistence in Luke's Gospel*. Grand Rapids: Eerdmans, 2012.

_____."You Just Don't Understand or Do You?" In *A Feminist Companion to John*. Vol. 1, edited by Amy-Jill Levine, 15–47. Cleveland: The Pilgrim Press, 2003.

Stibbe, Mark W.G. *John As Storyteller: Narrative Criticism and the Fourth Gospel*. Cambridge: University Press, 1992.

_____. *John's Gospel*. London: Routledge, 1994.

Story, J. Lyle. "Female and Male in Four Anointing Stories." *Priscilla Papers* 23 (2009): 16–23.

Stump, Elenore. *Wandering in Darkness: Narrative and the Problem of Suffering,* Oxford: Clarendeon Press, 2012

Sundermeier, Theo. "Martha hatte alle Hände voll zu tun." In *Dass Gott eine grosse Barmherzigkeit habe*, edited by Doris Hiller and Christine Gress, 236–241. Leipzig: Evangelische Verlagsanstalt, 2001.

Tannehill, Robert C. *Luke,* ANTC. Nashville: Abingdon Press, 1996.

Theissen, Gerd. *The Gospels in Context: Social and Political History in the Synoptic Tradition*. Minneapolis: fortress Press, 1991

Thomas, David. *The Gospel of John: Expository and Homiletical Commentary*. Grand Rapids: Kregel, 1980.

Tiede, David L. *Luke,* ACNT. Minneapolis: Augsburg, 1988.

Tovey, Derek. *Narrative Art and Act in the Fourth Gospel*. Sheffield: Sheffield Academic Press, 1997.

Vinson, Richard B. *Luke*. Macon: Symyth and Helwys, 2009.

Wall, Robert W. "Martha and Mary (Luke 10:38–42) in the Context of a Christian Deuteronomy." *JSNT* 35 (1989): 19–35.

Webster, Jane S. *Ingesting Jesus: Eating and Drinking in the Gospel of John*. Atlanta: Society of Biblical Literature, 2003.

Weima, Jeffery A. D. "Literary Criticism." In *Interpreting the New Testament: Essays on Methods and Issues,* edited by David Alan Black and David S. Dockery, 150–169. Nashville: Broadman and Holman, 2001

Whitacre, Rodney A. *John,* IVPNTC. Downers Grove: InterVarsity Press, 1999.

Witherington III, Ben. *The Acts of the Apostles: A Socio-Rhetorical Commentary.* Grand Rapids: Eerdmans, 1998.

_____.*John's Wisdom.* Louisville: Westminster John Knox Press, 1995.

_____.*Women in the Ministry of Jesus.* Cambridge: Cambridge University Press, 1984.

Yamaguchi, Satoko. *Mary & Martha: Women in the World of Jesus.* Maryknoll: Orbis Books, 2002.